WHY ME?

ROGER CARSWELL

WHY ME?

PERSONAL STORIES OF HOPE IN SUFFERING

Copyright © 1992 by Roger Carswell

First published in Great Britain in 1992,
this revised edition published in 2016.

Reprinted once

British Library Cataloguing in Publication Data
A record for this book is available from the British Library

ISBN: 978-1-910587-67-6

Designed and typeset by Pete Barnsley (Creative Hoot)

Printed and bound by CPI Group (UK) Ltd, Croydon, CR0 4YY

10Publishing, a division of 10ofthose.com
Unit C, Tomlinson Road, Leyland, Lancashire, PR25 2DY, England

Email: info@10ofthose.com
Website: www.10ofthose.com

DEDICATION

This book is dedicated to those who at this moment are suffering and enduring persecution simply for their faith in the Lord Jesus Christ. To those followers of Jesus who refuse to be silenced or intimidated into worshipping in a way they know is wrong, and to all Christians who are imprisoned or living in fear of what will happen to them or their families: though their stories may never be highlighted by the media or told this side of eternity, I dedicate this book with prayers and esteem.

APPRECIATION

Authentic Media first published *Why me?* in 1992. I am grateful to all who were involved in its production and distribution. My family, especially my wife, Dot, were very patient as I wrote the manuscript by hand and passed it on to Christine Watts to type it up. That book had several reprints but has now been out of print for some years.

However, a number of people asked me to try to have it reprinted, so I am grateful to 10Publishing for their enthusiasm to do so. I have tried to keep to the original manuscript, but there are parts where the book has been updated. As well, I have added four more stories, which increase the variety of people and situations being retold. I am grateful to all those whose stories have been written in this book, recognising that it can be painful to go over past events. There are many other people, whom I know well and who have similarly moving stories, but I have tried to cover a variety of situations and wanted to avoid being gratuitous or insensitive by including more.

I had the privilege of meeting and publicly interviewing Thomas H. Graumann in Nachod in the Czech Republic. His story is based on his publication, *The twice rescued child*. I am grateful to Jeanette Thorne of Wakefield for typing this for me, and to my wife, Dot, Janice Bowman of Wigston, Leicester, and

Michael Orr of Maryport for their helpful suggestions regarding the manuscript.

As a teenager on holiday in the Middle East I was introduced into a relationship with God through trusting Jesus as my Lord and Saviour. My deepest thanks will always go to Him for the grace, guidance and gladness He has faithfully showered on me. My desire is that this book will commend Him to you.

CONTENTS

INTRODUCTION

No one likes to suffer. Yet life is not fair. We wonder why it seems that the worst people prosper and the vulnerable struggle through no fault of their own. Most people would love to believe that if and when pain comes their way they would be courageous examples, bearing it with strength, patience and hope.

'Why me?' has chapters that briefly try to examine these issues. Sandwiched between them are 12 stories of people who have been through the mill of suffering, yet have either found or proved God in life's toughest times. Men and women, young and old, from different nations and backgrounds, each has suffered; some lingeringly, others suddenly and dramatically. They have heard the voice of God, so could trust Him in the silences. They have found that faith is not based on explanations but on the promises of God. Their testimonies challenge us to listen to the Lord of all, who is never taken by surprise, but is at work in all circumstances, personal and global.

Just over 600 years before Jesus was born, the prophet Habakkuk was perplexed, knowing that his country was about to be invaded by the cruel Babylonians. He could not understand why God was allowing this, but as he prayed, waiting for God and listening to Him, Habakkuk sang words which have been immortalised and sung in public worship since.

Though the fig tree may not blossom,
Nor fruit be on the vines;
Though the labour of the olive may fail,
And the fields yield no food;
Though the flock may be cut off from the fold,
And there be no herd in the stalls –
Yet I will rejoice in the LORD,
I will joy in the God of my salvation.
    (Habakkuk 3:17–18, NKJV)

In writing this book my prayer has been that you will find the God who not only cares for you, but can cope with you. We are invited to come to Him as we are, and as we respond, He does not leave us as we are, but works in us to make us the people we were created to be, and – in His time – to take us Home to be with Him for ever.

CHAPTER 1

WHY DOESN'T GOD INTERVENE?

For affliction does not come from the dust, Nor does trouble spring from the ground; Yet man is born to trouble, As the sparks fly upward. (Job 5:6–7, NKJV)

I had been waiting for some time at what was then the Czechoslovakian border for customs' control to allow me to drive into Austria. It was a beautiful sunny morning, but the gentleman in the car behind me looked gloomy and concerned. Eventually we struck up a conversation.

He was a German university lecturer and, like me, was returning from Poland. He had visited Auschwitz Concentration Camp, which is now a memorial to the unimaginable suffering of the 1930s and 40s. He felt overwhelmed with grief and shame. He too was a Christian, but found himself, as do so many others, asking himself, 'Why didn't God do something to stop it all?'

Over the centuries suffering has afflicted multitudes

of people. It is only decades since six million Jews were exterminated in the Holocaust. But there have been other holocausts. The first 20th-century genocide began in 1915 when in just six months 1,500,000 Armenians were killed. Since then millions of Soviet citizens died under the rule of Stalin. Between 20 and 50 million Chinese died under the rule of Chairman Mao. Names like Pol Pot, Idi Amin, Nicolae Ceausescu, Saddam Hussein, the dynasty of North Korean rulers, and ISIL strike terror into the hearts of bereft, beleaguered people.

The immediate causes of these and similar tragedies are clear. Human greed craves power, wealth and territory, which in turn leads to the suffering, loss and war. Far too often corrupt governments will stop at nothing to silence or eradicate those it perceives to be enemies of the state. It is reckoned by some, for example, that about 150,000 Christians are martyred each year for their faith.

Other people are left in a cycle of poverty and hopelessness because 'the system' overlooks or ignores their plight. Refugees and migrants have become a commonplace phenomena. Too often 'the innocent' are caught up in an inescapable trap through the wilfulness or wickedness of someone with a point to prove.

Sometimes though, human negligence is the cause of tragedy, be it flooding, a train crash or an unforeseen 'accident waiting to happen'.

And there are also apparently inexplicable tragedies. Disasters which occur on a national or global scale are regularly in our headlines. For a period of time the world's media focuses attention on these events, and compassion is aroused in the hearts of people across the continents. Debate and discussion follow with a view to preventing a recurrence of such disasters.

Despite this, they continue to happen. Millions die each year from malnutrition and starvation. We hear horrible statistics which mask the human pain of people dying through natural disasters, rampant epidemics, earthquakes, tsunamis, famines, cyclones, droughts and the like.

Pictures we see on our television screens frequently concentrate on the plight of an individual. We are shown the solitary child with his or her bloated belly and wasted limbs. We watch a hopeless family surveying their home and little land overwhelmed by floods. They remind us that communal disasters are, in fact, a series of individual tragedies.

Individual sadness is always nearby too. The situation may bypass the world's – or even the local – media, but bereavement, terminal illness, marital break-up, rebellious children, financial ruin and redundancy each have the power to deeply wound. Shattered dreams, disappointed hopes, broken hearts, as well as the problems of disease or old age, are close to all of us. It may be hard to enter into someone else's suffering when our own seems more than we can bear. We may feel like my eight-year-old son who, when he heard what I was writing asked, 'Will you tell them about what happened when I went over the handlebars of my bike?'

Whatever the source of the tragedy, no suffering is trivial. It is therefore natural that people should ask, 'Why doesn't God intervene?' However, when we ask a question like this the inference appears to be that all this suffering is somehow God's responsibility; that it is part and parcel of the world that He created. This is far from the truth. The opening chapters of the Bible – God's written message to humanity – show us clearly ...

The world as it was

We read that the Almighty God created the world in which we live. At the end of each day of creation He looked and saw that it was good. Six times we read in the opening chapter of the Bible's first book, Genesis, that what God had made was good. When He then created the first man and woman, we read, 'God saw all that He had made, and it was very good.'

It is impossible for us to imagine a world where there was no suffering, sin, disease or death. God created a paradise in which men and women could live in harmony with each other, and with Him. Everything in the universe was still supremely good. There was no struggle for existence, no environmental pollution, no poverty, no physical calamities, no tears shed in uncontrolled grief. Instead there was total freedom, exhilaration, joy and peace.

Clearly something has gone wrong. Sin, suffering and death have entered the world and the results have been cataclysmic. The world as it was has become ...

The world as it is

In a moment of time, by an act of deliberate rebellion, the first man and woman disobeyed their Creator, opening the door for evil to flood the world. It was not God's desire that we should discover evil in the world, but when we did everything was affected. A curse came upon the creation affecting animals, women, men and the elements themselves. The stage was now set for the long, sad history of humanity. Things designed for our benefit became instruments of blight.

The Bible shows us how the whole of creation is involved in this suffering, likening it to 'groaning in the pains of childbirth' (Romans 8:22). The Second Law of Thermodynamics, a basic law of science, teaches that all systems left to themselves tend to become disordered. Such is our world today.

We human beings, caught up in this world order, are born to suffering and eventually death. Peter Marshall, a former chaplain to the U.S. Senate, used to tell this story: 'A merchant in Baghdad one day sent his servant to the market. Before very long the servant returned, but was pale and trembling. In great agitation he said to his master, "Down in the market place I was jostled by a woman in the crowd, and when I turned around I saw she was called 'Death'. She looked at me and made a threatening gesture. Master, please lend me your horse, for I must hasten to avoid her. I will ride to Samara and there I will hide, and Death will not find me." The merchant lent him his horse, and the servant galloped away in great haste.

'Later, the merchant went down to the market and saw Death standing in the crowd. He asked her, "Why did you frighten my servant this morning? Why did you make threatening gestures?"

'"That was not a threatening gesture," Death replied. "It was only a start of surprise. I was astonished to see him in Baghdad, for I have an appointment with him tonight in Samara!"'

Louis Armstrong may have sung about 'a Wonderful World', but we know that all is not well. Instead, we hear about trouble in the Middle East, in Sudan, Nigeria, Bangladesh, Pakistan, the Far East and South Africa. The world is like an armless, legless, headless Greek sculpture on a museum plinth; we see beauty, but recognise that compared with its original state we are not seeing the splendour of what was originally made.

So when we ask why God allows suffering, we have to face the fact that the suffering is fundamentally the result of human rebellion and sin. Sometimes it may be the direct result. God, who is altogether loving, is also a just God, so there is always a penalty for sin. Sometimes that punishment seems to be withheld, even until after death, but at other times it is immediate. In the Bible we read how God judged nations, cities and individuals because of their continual refusal to obey His commands. If people flout God's laws, then somewhere along the line there will be suffering on a personal or communal scale. Everything we do has consequences.

However, although all suffering is the direct result of human rebellion against God, this does not mean that some particular incident is the result of a particular sin.

In John's Gospel chapter 9, Jesus was asked whether the sin of a blind man's parents or of the man himself had led to the blindness. Jesus responded saying that it was neither the sin of the man nor his parents that had brought about the blindness. The man was bound up in the bundle of life, but Jesus added that God would be glorified through it all.

The Bible also teaches us that the world will not always be torn apart by sin, suffering and strife. It points us to ...

The world as it will be

As it looks into the future, the Bible teaches us that the present troubles are, in themselves, a sign of the future time when Jesus will return to this earth, not as a baby in a manger, but as King of kings. He will bring judgement on all who do not know Him as Lord and Saviour, and reign with those who have trusted Him. Many Christians, looking at the signs the Bible says will be evident before Jesus' return, believe that that day is not far away.

The story is told of a child who heard the Town Hall clock chime at mid-day. It struck not 12 times, but 13. The child ran to his mother saying, 'Mummy, it's later than it has ever been before!' That is how our present times seem to many Bible scholars.

In the Bible – in 2 Timothy 3 – the early Christian leader, Paul, wrote, 'There will be terrible times in the last days. People will be lovers of themselves, lovers of money, boastful, proud, abusive, disobedient to their parents, ungrateful, unholy, without love, unforgiving, slanderous, without self-control, brutal, not lovers of the good, treacherous, rash, conceited, lovers of pleasure rather than lovers of God – having a form of godliness but denying its power ... always learning but never able to acknowledge the truth.'

In Matthew's Gospel chapter 24, we read of Jesus saying that some of the signs indicating the build up to the 'last days' would be wars and rumours of wars; famines, earthquakes and persecutions; false prophets, some even saying, 'I am the Christ' and some showing signs and wonders; lawlessness and then great tribulation. The decadence of our present age is foretold in the Bible and is one of the signs that the second coming of the Lord Jesus is getting nearer.

We also learn from the Bible that one day an eternal sentence will be passed on certain people. Gravestones often have engraved upon them the letters R.I.P. But there will be no rest for those who persistently refuse to accept the one and only way of salvation, which God has provided. Jesus, who was so full of love, consistently warned people of the necessity to turn from their sins and trust Him as the only one who can forgive a person and be with them, not only in this life but through eternity.

Near the end of the last of the 66 books of the Bible (the Book of Revelation), God underscores the everlasting penalty for those who refuse to receive God's mercy: 'The cowardly, the unbelieving, the vile, the murderers, the sexually immoral, those who practise magic arts, the idolaters and all liars – their place will be in the fiery lake of burning sulphur. This is the second death' (Revelation 21:8).

For those who are 'in Christ', who have trusted Him as their Lord and Saviour, trouble will cease at the moment of death or at the return of Jesus Christ. Anne Brontë, the novelist, said that for the believer 'death is but the doorway to eternal life'. The Christian looks forward to the time when 'God will wipe away every tear from their eyes; there shall be no more death, nor sorrow, nor crying. There shall be no more pain, for the former things have passed away' (Revelation 21:4 NKJV).

The paradise lost when sin entered the world will be a paradise regained. We read in the Bible of a new heaven and a new earth. Heaven is the home of God, and home for all those who have trusted Jesus and so know God as their Heavenly Father. Their place there has been purchased for them at the price of the blood of Jesus when He died on the cross. His death for sin is God's only means whereby the passport to heaven can be given to all those who receive it. Heaven is a gift, not a reward; the Bible says, 'For the wages of sin is death, but the gift of God is eternal life, life in Christ Jesus our Lord'. (Romans 6:23).

The journey may not always be smooth, but the end of the journey is always glorious.

CHAPTER 2

GOD INTERVENES – TO HIS OWN COST

What is man that You are mindful of him, And the son of man that You visit him? (Psalm 8:4, NKJV)

The world's oldest book is believed by many people to be the Book of Job in the Bible. We are not told who wrote it, but Lord Tennyson called it, 'The greatest poem, whether of ancient or modern literature.' It is fitting that this early book should deal with the oldest of problems: 'Why do the innocent suffer?'

The Book of Job opens with a scene in heaven where Satan, the supreme cynic, suggests to God Himself that Job obeys Him only because of the material prosperity that results from his devotion. Job never knew of this conversation, but in reply to the devil, God allowed Satan to take from Job his children, his business and eventually his health. Bereft, bankrupt and covered with boils, even Job's wife appeared to turn against him.

In all Job's dire sufferings, he never accused God of wrongdoing. In fact he said, 'Naked I came from my mother's womb, and naked I shall depart. The LORD gave and the LORD has taken away; may the name of the LORD be praised.' (Job 1:21). However, so dark was his experience and so unhelpful the words of his so-called 'comforters' that Job grappled with words and metaphors to try to express the anguish of his soul. In Job 19 he likened himself to an animal caught in a net (v.6); to a criminal in court (v.7); to a traveller stuck at a roadblock (v.8); to a dethroned king (v.9); to a building that is being demolished (v.10), to a tree being uprooted (v.10), and to an enemy being besieged by God (vv.11-12). He emotionally describes how his relatives and friends, servants and children all forsook, mocked and persecuted him.

Perhaps you find yourself identifying with Job. Maybe life is treating you harshly. Nobody understands you, and sometimes you don't really understand yourself. So is there any clear reason why God allows suffering?

First though, we need to remind ourselves that we are human beings – finite, fickle and often foolish. If we could understand all there is to know about God and our world, either we would not be human or God would not be God! It is significant that although we know the background to Job's story, he was never told why he had to endure such affliction. In the Bible we read, 'The secret things belong to the LORD our God, but the things revealed belong to us and to our children for ever, that we may follow all the words of the law' (Deuteronomy 29:29).

Through the centuries Christians have confronted the question of suffering. John Paton, pioneer missionary to the New Hebrides (now Vanuatu) had to dig the graves both of his only son and of his wife, and then sit on them until he knew their bodies would have decomposed, for he feared cannibals would dig up the bodies. He wrote in his journal in 1859: 'I do not pretend to see through the mystery of such visitations, but I do know that God is my Father.'

More recently is the experience of Dr. Helen Roseveare. Converted to Christ as a medical student at Cambridge University, she became a medical missionary in the Belgian Congo. After years of amazing service, during the Simba rebellion in 1964 she was captured, brutally treated and imprisoned. She has since asked Christians, 'Can you thank God that He trusts you with suffering, even if He never tells you why?'

We have already considered how individuals suffer through deliberate acts as well as through negligence. Events at Lockerbie; in Northern Ireland; in Syria; Iraq; Afghanistan; on a Tunisian beach, and dates like 9/11 and 7/7 all bear testimony to this.

Nearly 2,000 years ago two similar incidents were the subject of comment by Jesus. In the first, there had been a deliberate act of official terrorism in which Galileans were massacred in the temple while worshipping God. There was a religious and political atrocity ordered by the Roman Governor in charge of Judea, Pontius Pilate. It was a foolish act and helped to bring about Pilate's final downfall, but that did not help the people who were martyred in this cowardly act of violence. In the second incident, 18 people died when the Tower of Siloam collapsed. Whether this was because of faulty design or construction we can only guess. Despite the passing of years, the Bible is always relevant and topical.

Luke's Gospel records how people brought to Jesus news

of Pilate's massacre of the pilgrims. In reply Jesus drew two lessons and linked the two incidents. First, He says that in neither case did people suffer because of some particular sin they had committed. The guilty person in the massacre was Pilate. We are not told who was responsible for the collapse of the tower. The victims, like the man born blind of whom we read about in John 9, were caught up in the bundle of life. They were neither more innocent nor more guilty than any other people.

The second lesson that Jesus drew from the incidents was that they call us to repentance. Jesus said, 'Unless you repent, you too will all perish' (Luke 13:5). The theme of repentance runs through the whole Bible. Many of the prophets, who were preaching in the centuries before Jesus came, were calling the people to repent – to turn from their sinful ways and return to God. Repentance was the great theme of Jesus' cousin, John the Baptist. Jesus began His preaching ministry by calling people to repent. It was also at the heart of the first great Christian sermon preached by Peter shortly after the ascension of Jesus back to heaven. In fact every sermon recorded in the Book of Acts, which tells the story of the early church, has in it the theme of repentance. We all need to repent of our sin; we need to turn from all that is wrong and 'look to' Jesus to be our Lord and Saviour.

It is God Himself who has made such a turning and salvation possible. He did this when He seemed to stand aside from an evil situation and yet, at the same time, made that situation the greatest act of divine intervention. Have you ever wondered why, when Jesus was being crucified, God the Father did not intervene, and halt the horror of what was happening?

God had already stepped into the world He had made. When Jesus was born in Bethlehem, God was clothing Himself in humanity. The Creator was becoming like us, His creation. He took on Himself flesh and blood, being born, not in a mansion but laid in a manger, the son of a young virgin who was not yet married to Joseph. Jesus is as much God as God is God; and as much a man as any man is man! He is the God-man, who came 'to seek and to save those who are lost' (Luke 19:10, LEB) and to reconcile people to God. Throughout Jesus' three years of public ministry He was scorned and derided. While He went about doing good, giving speech to the mute, sight to the blind, hearing to the deaf, healing to the leper, strength to the lame, life to the dead, and forgiveness to the sinner, His enemies were plotting to kill Him. Eventually, the crowds turned out howling for His crucifixion.

Jesus suffered physically

His back was beaten with unnumbered lashings; they pulled His beard and spat in His face; they beat and buffeted Him, wedging a crown of thorns on His brow. Then on the lacerated back they compelled Him to carry a rough, rugged, Roman cross. Reaching a place called Calvary, they stretched out His body on the cross, nailing His hands and feet to the wood. Suspended on the cross, they left Him hanging, covered only with blood, sweat and dust, in the scorching heat of the Mediterranean sun. Searing pain, thirst, swarming flies and gasping for breath all intensified the suffering inflicted on the kindest, most loving, caring, compassionate 'Friend of Sinners'.

Jesus suffered emotionally

Jesus' disciples, who had once left everything to follow Him, now deserted Him and fled. Crowds who had heard the finest messages, who had been fed by His hand or healed, now mocked Jesus and watched Him being crucified. The disciples, scattering like frightened sheep, would have wounded the heart of Jesus who had given Himself unreservedly to them.

Jesus suffered spiritually

Throughout all eternity-past, Jesus had been at one with His Father and the Holy Spirit. The Father, Son and Holy Spirit – the triune God – had experienced total unity and love in their eternal relationship. God has revealed Himself in the Bible as being one God in three persons. And yet on the cross Jesus cried out, 'My God, my God, why have you forsaken me?' (Mark 15:34).

Throughout the last 2,000 years Christians have experienced the immediate presence of God, both in tough and good times. For example, Stephen, the first Christian martyr, after a farce of a trial was sentenced to be stoned to death. As the rocks pounded his body, Stephen looked up to see Jesus standing in heaven waiting to receive him. Paul, the great Christian missionary, just prior to his execution wrote, 'At my first defence, no-one came to my support, but everyone deserted me But the Lord stood at my side and gave me strength' (2 Timothy 4:16-17).

It was different for Jesus: the Gospels record seven sentences that Jesus spoke while on the cross. His first and His final words were spoken to God, His Father. But as the sin of the world was laid on Jesus, in deep anguish He addressed

God, not as His Father but, 'My God, my God, why have you forsaken me?' The evil, the wrong thoughts, words and deeds that have wrought havoc on our world, were carried by Jesus on the cross. And the Father, who is so pure that He cannot even look on sin, turned away from His own Son as He suffered and paid for our sin. He was forsaken by His Father, so that we could be forgiven and never forsaken by Him. Sin separates, but Jesus died in our place, taking that separation on Himself. Sin brings death and hell, but Jesus tasted death for everyone, taking our hell on Himself. I remember hearing a soloist sing the words, 'He could have called ten thousand angels To ... set Him free ... But He died alone for you and me.'

We can never plumb the depths that Jesus went through for us. To be cut off from His Father, to take on Himself our sin and die, is an experience deeper and darker than any other individual has ever had to go through. God the Father allowed His Son to suffer all this because there was no other way for His justice and love to be satisfied. Only through Jesus' substitutionary death can people be forgiven and reconciled to God. Calvary is primarily the place where God did intervene, at the cost of tremendous suffering to Himself.

While 'Good Friday' is the day traditionally set aside to remind us of the death of Jesus, we also have Easter Sunday. Jesus gave Himself over to death, but that was not the end of the story. Three days later He rose from the dead, having conquered the great conquerors, sin, death and the grave. He had defeated the root cause of all the trouble in the world. He can overcome the despair that people feel.

Because of what Jesus has accomplished for us on the cross,

we can be rescued from the overwhelming sense of despair and defeat experienced by Job, who lived long before Jesus was born. Job spoke of feeling trapped, but when a person trusts Jesus Christ as Lord and Saviour, He sets that person free. Jesus said, 'If the Son sets you free, you will be free indeed.' (John 8:36). Job thought of himself as a criminal, but the Apostle Paul could write of Christians, 'There is therefore now no condemnation to those who are in Christ Jesus' (Romans 8:1, NKJV).

The Christian believer need never feel that he or she is stuck at a roadblock. God promises to guide those who belong to Him. 'If the LORD delights in a man's way, he makes his steps firm' (Psalm 37:23). Rather than feeling like a dethroned king, those who receive Christ into their lives have a new power to do that which is right. In fact God looks at us in a new light, giving us the authority to live as we should, so that the Bible says of all Christians, '[You] have made us kings and priests to our God' (Revelation 5:10).

As soon as a person has accepted Jesus as their personal Lord and Saviour, God by His Holy Spirit comes to live within the life of that believer. Job thought of himself as a building being destroyed and as a tree being uprooted, but the experience of a Christian is that while the body grows old, becoming weak and weary, the innermost being – the soul – is being renewed (2 Corinthians 4:16). Job felt that he had become God's enemy, but all who repent and believe are reconciled to God through Jesus Christ (see Romans 5:10).

Job felt isolated, but God promises His eternal presence with us when we trust Him. The Christian can echo the words of the psalmist, 'When my father and my mother forsake me, then the LORD will take care of me' (Psalm 27:10).

The death of Jesus was seen at first by His disciples to be a catastrophe of untold proportions. But when Jesus rose from the dead they began to realise that this seeming tragedy was in fact God's major triumph, one in which all those who put their trust in Him can share.

The death of Jesus is an unforgettable event. Human tragedies pass from our minds, but the death of Jesus will never be forgotten. Christians meet regularly to celebrate what they call, 'The Lord's Supper'. They eat a portion of bread and drink a sip of wine as a deliberate reminder of the fact that Jesus' body was broken and His blood shed for us. We can never forget such a sacrifice, never forget that God has intervened at such tremendous cost to Himself.

We have seen that being a Christian is no guarantee of trouble-free living. For 2,000 years true believers have suffered in mind and body not only because of natural disasters and disease, but also at the hands of those who have persecuted them.

The world that hated Jesus has often hated His followers. It has been reckoned that the last century had more Christian martyrs than all the previous 19 added together. So many countries have governments which hound Christians, imprisoning and killing them. Believers are not immunised against the suffering of the world, where the innocent are often caught up in the consequences of the evil actions of others.

Christianity is more than crutch (though at times a crutch can be very useful!). God promises to be an ever-present help in time of trouble (Psalm 46:1). He is well able to meet the deepest needs of any individual. He is never caught out or taken by surprise. He has never uttered the words, 'I didn't expect that!'

Jesus spent His life bringing help to those in need. His miracles were not only signs of who He is, but genuine acts of love and compassion. However, He did not heal all whom He met. On one occasion, for example, Jesus went to the pool of Bethesda where there was 'a great multitude' (John 5:3, NKJV) of sick people. Yet Jesus healed only one paralysed man. We cannot explain why Jesus healed some but not others. We do believe, though, that He is altogether wise, loving and powerful.

There is one Bible sentence, or verse, which has brought comfort to countless Christians: 'And we know that all things work together for good to those who love God, to those who are the called according to His purpose' (Romans 8:28, NKJV). God never wastes any pain, tears, time or toil. To believe this is not simply to clutch at straws. It is the result of the Christian experience of those who rest upon what God has promised in His Word, the Bible.

In the following chapters are 12 stories of Christians who in different and often dramatic ways have suffered or are still suffering. All the stories are true, and each, apart from Ethel Waters are, or were, people I knew well. Ethel Waters and 'Lucy' have both died. I had the privilege of speaking at 'Lucy's' funeral in 2014.

Two themes shine through the darkness of their experiences. First, they have an overwhelming sense of God's presence with them, despite everything. Secondly, they have an unshakeable confidence and trust that God has a purpose in all that has happened, even though they may not have been able to explain everything at the time.

CHAPTER 3

BACK FROM 'THE DEAD'
THE STORY OF SARA WEBSTER

*Fear not, for I am with you; Be not dismayed, for I am
your God. I will strengthen you, Yes, I will help you, I
will uphold you with My righteous right hand.
(Isaiah 41:10, NKJV)*

'One perfect day several summers ago, I walked along a
quiet path near my Welsh home. It was a path I had run along
as a child. Now I had to take it more slowly with the help of a
walking stick. Yet, as I gazed up at the mountains, I thanked
God that I could walk at all. At 18 I'd contracted a severe form
of meningitis and both my legs had been amputated. Now I felt
I had finally made it back from a long and frightening journey.'
So says Sara Webster.

She was born in August 1968 in Wales. Both she and her
parents are fluent Welsh-speakers. She was a bright girl who
always wanted to be a doctor. At the age of 15 she passed 12
'O' levels, and two years later she was taking her 'A' levels.

However, the night before the first examination she suffered a slipped disc and ended up actually taking her 'A' level examinations on her back with an external examiner sitting in. The fact that Liverpool University Medical School accepted her application was proof to her that the Lord wanted her there. This was the first real drama of her life. Until then Sara was just a normal healthy girl enjoying cycling, swimming and squash. It was at a Christian camp that Sara had become a real Christian. Recalling what happened at the age of 14 she says,

'It was the first time that I had really heard the Christian gospel and realised that I was a sinner. I always thought that because I lived in what we called "a Christian country", and said the Lord's Prayer before I went to bed, tried to get my homework in on time and did not lie or steal, I was a Christian.

'Then at the camp I heard about Jesus, His death and resurrection, about heaven and hell, and that I needed to be "born again" so that Jesus would become a reality in my life, and I could enjoy a personal relationship with God. As a young girl it sort of frightened me and made me realise that as I was, I was going to hell. But the message about Jesus the Saviour, and a loving God who sent His Son to die for all of us at Calvary, reassured me. Understanding that Jesus loved me as I was, and had taken the punishment for my sins on the cross gave me such joy and security. I prayed a prayer that night asking Jesus, by the Holy Spirit, to come into my life, to forgive my sins and take control of me to make me whatever He wanted me to be.

'The following morning I told the leader of the camp about it. I can remember asking everyone to sing the chorus, "I have decided to follow Jesus". That really became my sort of motto, and there was no turning back.'

Sara remembers talking to a Christian friend at Liverpool University and saying, 'I don't know why the Lord has brought me to Liverpool, but I know there is a reason for it.' She has often been reminded of that since, believing that the reason was revealed when she became ill. What happened next she tells us in her own words.

'I was very excited when I went up to university. It was a new chapter of my life, with independence from home, being my own person, developing my own character. I had to stand on my own two feet, and start taking responsibility for my actions, being organised and planning my life. I felt I had to take my stand as a Christian since there were so many temptations around. Everyone else was living their own life, going to clubs and pubs, so it took me a while to work out where I wanted to go and whether I wanted to give in totally to God. One thing I found excellent while I was there was that I could go into so many churches in Liverpool and hear the gospel, because at home we had to travel some way to find a gospel-believing church. On the Sunday before I became ill I can remember walking down a road and seeing a road sign saying, "Changed priorities ahead". It made a real impression on me. I knew that though I was trying my best to live a Christian life and to honour the Lord, there was something wrong, and I was just holding back that little bit. It was as if God was saying to me, "No, you have to give in completely to me." Seeing that sign made me realise that God has to be first and I have to give Him 100%. That night I sincerely prayed that God would change me and make me the person that He would have me be. I wanted to be more useful to God. I never thought when I prayed that particular prayer how He would change me and how dramatic the outward change would be. It was the following Wednesday that I was taken ill.

'I had had a good day at the university. I had an exam on the Thursday so I was working hard that night. I phoned home and told my mum I had a light sore throat, but during the night the sore throat became worse. I started vomiting and gradually became more and more ill. I was taken to the university sick bay and eventually that night the doctor came and diagnosed meningitis. I was rushed to an infectious diseases hospital in Liverpool. I arrived there and subsequently had two cardiac arrests. So I suppose theoretically I died twice. But they resuscitated me. My parents were called from Wales. It must have been a terrible shock to them when the doctor said, "Your daughter is seriously ill and we think she might even be dying. Can you get over here as quickly as possible?" They naturally came straightaway, but that night I just seemed to grow weaker.

'I was very aware of what was happening and my mum often tells me that I would swing my legs over the bed and bang them on the floor. I kept on saying, "Rub my legs, rub my legs, I can feel the blood clotting." Even though my parents were told when they arrived that I had perhaps about half an hour to live, I managed miraculously to survive that night. The following day I went into respiratory failure and needed a life support machine for over six weeks. I stayed in that hospital for two days, but then my kidneys failed and I needed dialysis equipment. I was transferred to yet another hospital to be put on a dialysis machine. My liver then failed and everything seemed hopeless.

My condition just deteriorated. The doctors said the situation was very serious. Ten days into my illness they decided, as a last resort, to amputate both my legs below the knee.

'I was in a coma at this time, and it seemed that my life was just hanging by a thread, but I know that God was in control. When I became a Christian He promised never to leave me nor forsake me. He was in control of my life and had a specific plan for it: even when I was on that life support machine and everyone had given up hope, and the situation seemed so, so hopeless, He was there and sustained me and was in control. Thousands of God's people prayed and I really believed that it is by God's grace and Him powerfully answering prayers that I am here today.

'I came round six weeks later to discover that I no longer had any feet, and at that time, because of the drugs I was on, my memory was very poor, so they had to keep on telling me that I had lost my legs. Then one night, in the middle of the night, it really dawned on me what had happened. My parents had gone home for a couple of hours' sleep, so I asked the nurse to call them. They came, and I actually told them then what had happened, that I had lost my legs. It seemed as if it was my way of coping with it. I cannot deny it was a shock, but I was so thankful to be alive. I realised how ill I had been and God was so real to me in that Intensive Care Unit. It was as if Jesus Himself was there standing at the end of the bed, whenever I was lonely and desperate or worried about the future, and asking whether I would ever walk again. God gave me the peace that I needed so that I became thankful for little things and appreciated life for what it was. Things like being able to keep some food down, or eating jelly became such a blessing in a way. I think that has really taught me that in our lives from day to day we have to be thankful and must live one day at a time. A few weeks later I was taken down onto a general ward and I remained in hospital for seven months in all because I had to learn to walk again.

'Learning to walk on artificial legs is quite a long process and because I was very weak at the time, it was very hard. I had lost weight and was about 5½ stones (35kgs) then. But I just knew that I had to walk. If I wanted to be useful to God and to anyone again, I had to give it a go. It was very experimental in the first stages. I didn't decide, "Yes, I am going to walk again." It was, "Come on let's see if you can", and I can remember the first day they asked me to walk just a few steps. I actually walked about 10 feet (which was such a distance), and then gradually day after day, and week after week, I became stronger and more able to walk. Eventually, in the gym I was given a pair of legs that actually looked like legs, and I started walking with sticks. Even then God was with me and daily He gave me the strength and the courage to keep on going. He gave me, as well, the inner strength not to become bitter. Many things happened during that time in hospital. People said things that maybe they didn't mean, but nevertheless they really upset me at the time.'

Sara has a quiet confidence that even if she has to be on artificial legs for 60 or 70 years, ultimately it does not matter when compared with eternity and the certainty that heaven is her eternal home. The thought of being with Christ, where there will be no more pain, trials or burdens to carry was what kept her going in the early days and still does today.

Not everything was easy. One man receiving physiotherapy who had had amputations in exactly the same place said to her one day, 'Oh, who will marry you, girl? Your dancing days are over, aren't they?' She was very fragile at that time, and just sat in her wheelchair, wheeled herself to the hospital chapel and wept. Even then, God undertook because there was a Christian doctor at the Royal, whom she had never met before, but who came in just then. He was an older man and he put his arm around her, and said, 'It's alright now, I'm here.' Sara says, 'It was so strange. It seemed to me that it was as if the Lord Himself was saying to me "I'm here."' She has not seen that doctor since, but that day he was a real help and encouragement to her.

When things get out of perspective now, and little things become big issues, her remedy is a good cry, a good pray, and a good night's sleep. In that order! Sara has found that Satan – the devil – knows when to get at a person. He knows when we are weak, and it is at those times we can turn back to the Bible, reminding ourselves that Jesus died on the cross, and get life in perspective again, realising that ultimately, none of this matters. Speaking to herself she says reassuringly, 'Ok, your legs are hurting. Ok, you've had a horrible day. Ok, things have been awful, but ultimately all that matters is that you are safe for eternity, and that you are on your way "Home". It is only a matter of time, and the Lord will come back soon, and that is what we need to be ready for.'

At the time of her illness, there was national interest in Sara. *The Liverpool Echo*, the *Sunday Telegraph*, the *Sunday Times* and *Bella magazine*, as well as Welsh television told her story.

Now time has passed. Since the illness, Sara has passed her driving test learning to drive with hand controls, she returned to medical school and completed her course to become a General Practitioner. And of course, she has artificial legs. 'I didn't have a clue what an artificial leg looked like and I was so scared at the prospect of what I thought were just going to be big callipers. But a girl who was a fourth-year medical student walked into the Intensive Care Unit and said, "I'm an amputee. Can you tell which leg is mine and which is artificial?" And I couldn't. I was worried about how I could get my tights on and off and just little things like that, and she knew and could explain. She really helped me during that time.'

On 17 August 1991 Sara married David, a fellow doctor. They had met at the first Saturday night's Christian Union meeting in Liverpool University in her first year. She thought he was great but a bit unattainable for her! But they got to know each other. He came and visited her and even when she was on a life support machine he used to go and look through the window. He earnestly prayed for her, and encouraged the Christian Union people to do the same. He continued regularly visiting her, and they gradually became closer.

On the first Sunday Sara was allowed out of hospital she wanted to go to church. She was still in her wheelchair and together with her family she went to their church where they put on a thanksgiving service because she was there. David, a competent guitarist and singer, sang a solo, which meant so much to her. 'Like any other Christian couple, we can say that the Lord put us together. I can look back on these past years and feel I would never have got this far if the Lord had not gone before and prepared the way for me. He has brought me this far and He is not going to let me go now. He is the same yesterday, today and forever, and no matter what happens to us in the future we know that He is faithful, because He has proved His love for us in that Jesus died on Calvary. We should never ask God to prove His love for us again. I can say that He has proved His promises and that He will never leave me nor forsake me.

'He is my God and He is faithful. Jesus is a friend who sticks closer than a brother and will never let me down. He knows exactly how I feel when I am rock bottom. It is then that He gives me all that I need. He gives me the grace and the strength just to cope with my situation. Most importantly I have this inner life, and I am on my way to heaven. One day I will be there and see my Saviour's face. Just seeing Him and the beauty of heaven is going to be worth all the pain and suffering and the trials, and every tear that I have shed here on earth is going to be wiped away. Then I believe God is going to give me a new pair of legs, and the best pair ever! I am going to do things I have missed here, like running up and down stairs, and things like that. Ultimately, I think I will be so taken up with Him that I won't be concerned about anything else.

'I think that even if the Lord sat me down today and explained why it all happened I would not be able to understand. It is only then when I will be made like Jesus that I will understand, but then I won't need the answers because I will just be so happy to be there, and it will all have been worth it.'

CHAPTER 4

HIS EYE IS ON THE SPARROW

THE STORY OF ETHEL WATERS

He also brought me up out of a horrible pit, Out of the miry clay, And set my feet upon a rock, And established my steps. He has put a new song in my mouth – Praise to our God; Many will see it and fear, And will trust in the LORD. (Psalm 40:2–3, NKJV)

Jazz originated in the African-American communities in the late 19th and early 20th centuries. It makes heavy use of improvisation, polyrhythm, syncopation and the swung note. Jazz is one of America's original art forms. The story of Ethel Waters is typical of many famous jazz musicians, but has a feature which is touching and relevant.

Born in 1896, Ethel Waters was an African-American blues, pop and jazz singer and dramatic actress whose singing, based in blues tradition, featured her full-bodied voice and slow vibrato.

She was the first black entertainer to move successfully from the vaudeville and nightclub circuits to what blacks called 'the white time'. Reflecting on those days Ethel said, 'I used to work from nine 'til unconsciousness.'

Matching her vocal resources with an innate theatrical flair, Ethel projected the character and situation of every song she performed. But life was tough, often travelling on freight trains between gigs. Her friends, who were fiercely loyal to their friends, were thieves to anyone else. Ethel Waters performed regularly with Duke Ellington, Louis Armstrong and Fletcher Henderson. She had 50 hit records by 1933, topping the US charts in 1927 and 1931.

As an actress she was nominated for an Oscar in 1949, and won the New York Drama Critics Award for best actress in 1950. Breaking racial barriers she was the first black actress to play in a Broadway show (1939), and the first black singer to broadcast on radio (21 April 1922).

Ethel Waters was born in Chester, Pennsylvania to her 13-year-old mother who had been raped at knifepoint by John Waters, a mixed-race pianist who was a family acquaintance. He played no part in raising Ethel, who grew up in poverty, never living in the same place for more than 15 months. She said in one of her autobiographies, 'I was never a child. I was never cuddled or liked or understood by my family. I never felt I belonged. I was always an outsider.' She said, 'We never had a bath tub. Mom would bathe me in the wooden or tin washtub in the kitchen, or in a big lard can.' Because of the manner of her birth, her mother found it hard to accept her so she was brought up by various relatives.

Her mother, though, was the greatest influence on her life, and wanted to save her from the vice, lust and drinking that was all around her. Seeing the bad effect of drink and drugs on others, Ethel avoided them. Sharing a bedroom with several others, she saw things which were unhelpful for a young girl.

Ethel first married at the age of 13, but soon left her abusive husband. She attended school for just a few years and said, 'I have reason to be shy. I've been hurt plenty.'

Ethel sang in church when she was only five, but her professional singing debut took place in Philadelphia under the name Sweet Mama String Bean because of her physical appearance – she was scrawny and nearly six feet tall.

Around the age of 12, she experienced what she called a spiritual awakening. In the Mission Hall which she attended with her mother, she came to understand that she needed to find forgiveness and peace with God. Simply believing that Jesus had suffered and died on the cross paying the penalty for her sin, she prayed asking Jesus to live in her life.

A couple of years later though, she got into a fight with a white girl at the church, and never went back there. Although always conscious of God, she ceased to follow Him.

On her 17th birthday, while working as a low-paid maid, she attended a party and sang a ballad, captivated the audience and was offered work as a professional singer. Dozens of people later claimed to have 'discovered' her, which irritated Ethel! Her rendition of 'St. Louis Blues' was to become a classic.

Married and divorced three times, she was often seen fighting in public and found it hard to maintain friendships. Hurt by the racial prejudice of those around her, the music reflected the heartache and pain. She said, 'A song is a story – that's how it is to me – and I sing it so it tells the story.' Her audience were always made to feel her emotion.

Despite living a lavish life and having immense success, she questioned the meaningfulness of her life and career. Long ago, there had been a time when God was real to her and she trusted in Jesus. Believing in Jesus was one thing, but she was not experiencing His power in her life. Whilst performing in New York in 1957, she appeared on a television talk show, and was asked how she felt about the evangelist Billy Graham who was preaching in New York at that time. In her reply she said that the venture would be 'a success because God didn't sponsor flops'. Later she was asked to attend and hear him preach about the love of Jesus to sinners.

There were tens of thousands of people in the Madison Square Garden to hear Billy Graham, but as she listened 'I found it was a fulfilment of something I had been seeking for years. I was converted when I was 12 years old and in all honesty I strayed away. But once you give your life to our precious Saviour … He's there! Fame, fortune and success – nothing is like the satisfaction of something that happens in your life when Christ first enters it. I felt just like the prodigal son would have felt … I got to the place where I was so low but I let the Lord clean it up.' She rededicated her life to Jesus Christ, asking Him to be her Lord. Believing that Jesus had died paying the penalty for all her sin, and carrying all her hurt and pain, she asked Jesus to forgive all her past. The prayer was answered and the risen, living Jesus changed everything. She loved reading the Bible and telling others of Jesus.

Ethel Waters became a greatly esteemed member of the Billy Graham team, singing gospel songs at his huge events across the world. Her favourite song was 'His eye is on the sparrow, and I know He watches me'. (You can hear on YouTube Ethel Waters singing the song). At the age of 81, in 1977, Ethel Waters died of cancer. She went to be with her Lord, because heaven is not a reward for being good, but a gift purchased by Jesus and offered to everyone. Ethel Waters received that gift and revelled in it.

Speaking of black people, she said they 'are human beings with exactly the same faults and virtues as members of the other races'. But she knew too that Jesus came into the world not to call the righteous, but sinners to repentance. And she knew she qualified, as do we all!

Decades after her death, three of Ethel Waters' singles were inducted into the Grammy Hall of Fame: 'Dinah' in 1998 for Traditional Pop; 'Stormy Weather' in 2003 for Jazz, and 'Am I Blue?' in 2007 for Traditional Pop. And the USA postal service featured her on a stamp.

CHAPTER 5

THE TWICE RESCUED CHILD

THE STORY OF THOMAS H. GRAUMANN

Though my father and mother forsake me,
the Lord will receive me. (Psalm 27:10)

Thomas H. Graumann is a Czech Jew, naturalised American, Christian missionary to the Philippines and one of the 669 children rescued by Sir Nicholas Winton.

He was born in the town of Brno in Czechoslovakia in 1931 to a Jewish family. His father, Francis Graumann, made and sold shoes. His family was an assimilated secular family. Shortly after his brother Tony was born, his parents divorced and his mother, Frances, married Julius Hochberg. They moved to the village of Tesany, 15 miles outside of Brno, where his mother and stepfather were managers of a big estate.

After Hitler annexed Austria to Germany, his stepfather's

sister, Aunt Kamila, and her family arrived from Vienna and lived with the family while they were waiting for immigration papers to live in Australia. They warned Thomas' family that it was dangerous to stay in Europe, but they decided to stay and take care of their business where they knew best.

When Thomas was coming home one evening, he noticed a Nazi tank stuck in a ditch in front of their house. As a seven-year-old boy he was interested in the tank. He watched as the soldiers were pulling it out, but he was unaware of all that was going on in his stepfather's office. The Nazis had brought an ultimatum to evacuate Sudetenland. (The Munich Agreement of 1938, signed by Neville Chamberlain, President Deladier of France and Benito Mussolini of Italy gave the defended border region and its steel and coal industry to Hitler.) The commanding officer took over a room in their house and organised his unit from there. Thomas clearly remembers the other Nazis living in the village going up and down the streets on their motorcycles with sidecars. People watched them from the side of the road, and if they got too close to the road, the Nazis would knock them down and think this was great fun. Thomas' mother warned Tony and him not to go anywhere near them.

One day his mother took him to Brno to go to the theatre. They saw a gang of thugs along the road knocking down Jews, beating them up and breaking the display windows of Jewish shops. His mother took him to stand beside the armed guard at the door of the theatre. For that moment he felt very safe. As soon as the thugs passed though, they went home without attending the theatre. This was a very frightening situation. Hitler had said, 'If you give me Sudetenland, I will not ask for any more territory.'

But five months later, without resistance, Hitler marched into Prague, announced the Protectorate of Bohemia and Moravia, while Slovakia became an independent satellite of Germany.

Recalling what unfolded next, Thomas says, 'I remember the pastor of the evangelical church in the next village visiting us. He had studied in Edinburgh and apparently made a contact for us in Scotland. My mother started going to his church and later joined the church. Possibly through him, Mom contacted Nicholas Winton, sent him my photo and completed the application papers.

'Karel, our driver, took me to Brno to say goodbye to my father. His shop was full of Nazi soldiers. They liked his custom-made boots. There were more workers in the factory behind his shop. By this time he had his main shop in Brno with branches in Prague and Karlovy Vary. After I went to Scotland someone reported that my dad was a Jew, and I have been told that he committed suicide, but I have not seen this documented.'

Thomas' mother and grandma took him to the Prague Wilson Railway Station. There he was given a travel document; the number 652 was tied round his neck. He had two suitcases with clothes and a bag with food to eat along the way. As a young boy, he was excited to leave on this adventure. He probably left his mother in tears and distraught. She was only 29 when she said goodbye to him. She told him, 'Go to Britain, learn English and in a few months everything will be fine and you will be able to come home. When you grow up you may be able to represent your father's shoe company in London.'

First of all he was taken for a few days to the Priory at Selkirk, on the English/Scottish border, then for a short time he stayed at the home of a Rev. Sawyer. But when Mr. Sawyer was called up to the Army as a chaplain, Thomas was sent to the village of Connel on the shore of Loch Etive in the Western Highlands of Scotland. Mary Corson, a home economics teacher, welcomed Thomas and a boy called Tom Schlesinger to her home. Her sister, brother-in-law and cousin all went to meet them at the station, which was just five minutes walk from her home. Next door was the two-roomed village school where Thomas played with his new classmates and listened to lessons in the classroom for grades 1-5. He soon learned English and forgot Czech and German. At first his mother wrote to him every week, then by 1941 there were only one-line messages through the Red Cross. Then there was nothing.

There was little entertainment in the village, so when R. Hudson Pope, a greatly loved children's evangelist who for over 50 years worked with Scripture Union, came and conducted meetings for children, everyone in the village went to hear him. He would tell Bible stories and illustrated stories from John Bunyan's *Pilgrim's Progress*. There Thomas heard about Jesus and His invitation to children to come to God through Him. Thomas was assured that he would not be turned away, but that God loved him so much that He sent His Son to die in his place for his sins. When he understood that, this young orphan – for by now both his parents had died – bowed his head and prayed the words of a song,

Come into my heart, Lord Jesus,
Come in today
Come in to stay.
Come into my heart, Lord Jesus.

He was given a Scripture Union Card with Bible verses to read each day because he knew he needed to read the Bible if he was to grow spiritually.

In his reading one day he came to Exodus 13:2: 'Consecrate to me every firstborn male. The first offspring of every womb among the Israelites belongs to me, whether man or animal.' He knew he was the firstborn of a Jewish family, so he saw that God claimed him for Himself. Thomas says, 'I had been rescued by Nicholas Winton from almost certain death in a concentration camp with my mother and brother. By receiving Jesus I was rescued spiritually, so I owe my life to Nicholas Winton and I wanted to live for Jesus and help anyone I could.'

At the end of the war his Uncle Beda, who had been in London, returned to Prague with a Dr. Benes, and the Czech Government, which had been in exile. Dr Benes had previously advised his own and Thomas' family to stay in Czechoslovakia when he joined the army. On his return he wrote a letter to Thomas saying, 'All our relatives who remained in Czechoslovakia died in a concentration camp.' All through the war Thomas had been looking forward to returning to his home and his family. Though still young, he prayed and asked God to forgive the Nazis for what they had done to his family, and the bitterness was ultimately removed from his heart.

Eventually, Thomas trained to be a nurse and worked for eight years in the Philippine jungles as a missionary with the Overseas Missionary Fellowship. There he met and married Caroline. They now have four children and 10 grandchildren who all live near each other in Littleton, Colorado. While raising their own family and working as nurses they were an American family to students studying English at Spring International an American agency. They also sponsored refugees from Laos, Eritrea and Russia.

After the Velvet Revolution Thomas' grandmother's house was returned to his family. His cousin, Honza Horsky, born after the war, wrote to him about the house and Thomas and Caroline decided to return to the land of his birth. He retired from nursing and started teaching English. After 60 years, he finally discovered the man whom his mother had contacted and who had rescued him. He has had the opportunity to tell his story to many thousands of people and show the documentary of his life, *The Power of Good*, in schools, museums, churches and gatherings all over the Czech Republic and parts of the USA.

CHAPTER 6

THE DEATH OF A GOOD SAMARITAN
THE STORY OF RICHARD GARNHAM

Even though I walk through the valley of the shadow of death, I will fear no evil, for you are with me; your rod and your staff, they comfort me. (Psalm 23:4)

Richard is the minister of a large Baptist church in Northern Ireland. He is married to Elaine, and they have one son. He was brought up in a godly home and taught about God from being a small child. It was as a youngster that he personally asked Jesus to be his Lord and Saviour, after being challenged in a metalwork room at school as to whether he was a real Christian. Though far from being wild or wicked, he feared the prospect of hell if he were to die without trusting the Saviour. He had been taught and believed that Jesus had died and had risen again. That night he knelt by his bedside and asked Jesus to be his Saviour. He says that that night he had the best night's sleep because he knew he had peace with God, and the peace of God in his heart.

The decision he made, though, was no guarantee that life would be problem-free. Every year 16 January is deeply significant for Richard. He explains why:

'I belong to a very musical family. My dad was in the brass band. We always had friendly arguments because I was an enthusiastic pipe band man. We did a lot of singing together as a family, and Mum and Dad went out to different churches all over Northern Ireland singing together, for the glory of God. Often the entire family of two boys and two girls would join them. As well, we had many good times singing together in the home. We were looked upon as a singing family with musical talent. On 16 January there was a real tragedy for our family.

'It was a very cold and windy day. Snow was lying on the ground as I made my way to work. I was working as a body builder (cars!) in Dromara, miles away from my home. I tried to get there, but couldn't as my car was skidding and sliding dangerously in the snow.

'I returned home and was idly hanging about town when I saw the Fire Brigade return from a call. As a fire officer, my father had just coordinated the rescue of two ambulance men trapped in their vehicle by a fallen tree. Shortly after, the Fire Brigade was called out again to a similar accident where a tree had fallen on a car. This time I followed the fire engine with its gripping chains on the wheels, bells jangling and siren blaring – sounds I have always loved.

'The Fire Brigade had been trying to contact my father, but this time there was no reply from his call signal, "Bravo 1-3", for my father had been killed in the very car they were trying to reach. They were trying to get him to go to his own accident.

'As we approached a corner, 200 yards from the accident, I was prevented from going any further by another fallen tree. I believe this to have been the Lord's intervention to shield me from what would have been an unimaginable and unforgettable experience.

'I headed for home, expecting my father to pass me in his command car on his way to the accident. At home my mother asked me if I had seen my father because headquarters were looking for him. I said, "No" and just sat down and was going to prepare my lesson for the next week's Sunday school.

'Later, there was a knock on the door and two dark, uniformed figures stood there. I looked and thought it was my father coming home and bringing a colleague with him for dinner, as he sometimes did. However, it turned out that one was the Chief Fire Officer of Northern Ireland and the other his deputy. As soon as I saw the two of them I knew what they had come to say. They had the tragic news that my father had been killed. One of them took my arm for fear that I might faint; but something wonderful happened. I felt the arms of the Lord around me in a way I had never experienced before in my life.

'I remember the officer asking, "Where's your mother?" She was down in the basement doing the washing, and singing away. He asked me to go and get the next-door neighbour to come in and comfort my mother. I did so, but the neighbour went into hysterics and my mother ended up comforting her! I clearly recall my mother in the basement with the two men. They told her the bad news that her husband had been killed. She immediately replied by quoting the Bible, "The Lord has given and the Lord has taken away; blessed be the name of the Lord." There was never a finger of accusation pointed at the Lord and the singing didn't stop.'

As is the Northern Irish custom, the body of Richard's father, Reggie, was brought home, and different people came to visit. They came from all over the British Isles and from the Republic of Ireland. Courageously, through many tears, Richard's family were able to tell them of the Lord who was present even in the worst situations. A group of men came from the Fire Station where Station Officer Reggie Garnham had been in charge. They all went to the room where his body lay, but Richard said, "Look lads, all stand, and I'll pray for us." He put one arm round one man, and the other arm round another man and prayed, thanking God for his father and his influences on each of those men. He prayed that one day each of his father's colleagues would come to know Jesus as his father did. The prayer was answered in the life of one of those men that very day.

Richard's mother, Elaine, woke up in the middle of the night a day or so before the funeral and felt that the Lord was asking her and the family to sing at the funeral. She remembered how they been singing for many years when everything was going well, so why should they cease just because tragedy had struck? She put it to the family, wondering how they would react. Richard asked his mother what piece they would sing at the funeral. He went to his father's room and there was a music book with a marker in it, at the song:

> *All your anxiety, all your care*
> *Bring to the Saviour's feet*
> *Leave it there.*

That was the song that they as a family sang at the deeply moving funeral service. God was present with them. The church was absolutely packed out, and of course many fire officers, who had grown to love Reggie Garnham over the years, attended the service. Recently Richard met a man who said, 'To my dying day I will never forget that funeral.'

Reflecting on this, Richard asks himself, 'When I die, how will I be remembered? Will it be for the gossip I have passed on, or as one who influenced others for the Lord? I believe my father was one who influenced many others for the Lord.' That is what he was known for. In fact the headline of the local newspaper called him "The Good Samaritan".

Richard is convinced that his father is in heaven now, not because he was good, but because all his sin had been paid for by the Lord Jesus on the cross. Jesus alone can make a person fit for heaven. 'My father trusted in that, and now I want everyone to know this same good news.

'Just before my father died he bought a plaque which said,

> *Only one life,*
> *'Twill soon be past.*
> *Only what's done for Christ*
> *Will last.*

'I remember the Lord speaking very clearly to me through those words. I was brought face to face with the Lord saying in effect, "You've only one life, Richard. It will soon be past, and what are you going to do with it?" In response I prayed to God, saying, "Lord, you can take my life and use it."'

Soon after, in response to what clearly seemed God's leading, Richard left body building and started in full-time Christian service, first with a Christian organisation based in Northern Ireland and then in the Baptist ministry. He muses, 'I believe that were it not for the death of my father, I would not be in full-time Christian work today.'

CHAPTER 7

A SHATTERED FAMILY
THE STORY OF 'LUCY'

(Christian names have been changed in this story)

He heals the broken-hearted and binds up their
wounds. (Psalm 147:3)

Lucy was one of four children brought up in a non-Christian home. Her mother died when she was just 12. As a child Lucy had gone to church, but Jesus was to her only a good character of history.

When she was in her late teens, her father attended a mission where for a fortnight the gospel was preached in their local church. Several people came to put their trust in Jesus as Lord and Saviour in a way that was to not only turn their lives upside down, but would transform the church too. One night Lucy's father came home telling the children that he had been converted to Christ. It was Lucy's first real contact with the Christian message. But she couldn't help notice a new joy about her father. He started to sing hymns and was altogether a lovelier man to have as head of the home.

Lucy got to know the daughter of the minister of the church who also seemed to have a peace and joy about her life, which she said was because she knew God in a personal way. She explained to Lucy that she had a relationship with Jesus, and that He was not only a real person of history, but also someone who could be known today. All this started Lucy thinking about life: where we had come from; what we were doing; where we would go after death. If God was so real and powerful, she wanted to know Him.

She was 17 when one Saturday night Lucy went on a coach to a town-wide mission where again the gospel was being proclaimed. An evangelist from Northern Ireland was preaching on the theme of the danger of 'sitting on the fence' with regard to God. By this time, she had become quite familiar with the Christian message and the claims that Jesus had on her life. After all, He loved her and had died for her sin, and had risen from the dead. She knew that the most reasonable response was to put her trust in Jesus as Lord and Saviour, but she was still hesitant about what seemed to her to be taking such a huge step. But that evening the evangelist invited people to pray, confessing their sin to God, and trusting Him to forgive them and make their life new. Lucy thanked Jesus for dying for her and asked Him to come to live in her life. As she left the meeting to go back to the coach she thought, 'God is out here; He is everywhere, but best of all, He is in me!'

Immediately she sensed a peace, knowing the actual presence of the Lord with her. Now she wanted to live to please

God, rather than simply doing what everyone else was doing, and living for herself.

When she left school Lucy worked as a secretary for a short while, but at the age of 19 she fulfilled a long-time ambition to join the police force. She worked mainly with children, young people and women whilst working 'on the beat'. Later, she worked with the traffic police and an accident unit. She loved her job and was involved in inter-church youth work as well as being active in her church. She was vivacious with a mischievous streak that endeared her to everyone. She always had stories to tell, and loved to winsomely share with others what Jesus meant to her.

Her life was to change at the age of 21 when, during a police car chase, she had a collision with a heavy goods vehicle. She suffered what appeared to be straightforward whiplash injuries. At this time she did not even have time off work, thinking that nothing serious had happened to her, but it seems the effects and long-term implications became obvious much later.

As Lucy's Christian faith was becoming stronger she applied for, and was granted, six months, unpaid leave to go to a Bible college. She loved her time there. Upon returning to the police force she was transferred to another police station, and it was there that she met Richard. He was on the same shift as Lucy, and in the course of duty they got to know each other. She grew to like him, but didn't want to get involved with someone who didn't enjoy the same relationship with God. This relationship is what defined her as a person, meaning more to her than anything else, so how could she share her life with someone who didn't have the same priorities?

In time, Richard went to a gospel mission which was being held locally in a large marquee. There was no pressure to make a commitment to Christ, but Richard made a profession of faith in Jesus as his Lord and Saviour. Lucy had stressed to Richard that she didn't want him to become a believer just to please her. She wanted him to be a genuine Christian. He appeared to be sincere, getting involved in church and saying that he did trust Jesus. Richard and Lucy started dating and eventually married. It was a Christian wedding, full of police guests ... and a well-known criminal who had been converted and transformed while serving time in Dartmoor!

Two years later Lucy started to have problems with walking. She had not been born with any deformity of the back, so the medical consultant traced the cause to the accident of some years earlier. She needed major surgery on her back, and as a result had to leave her beloved police force.

She and Richard had two daughters. However, Lucy still had difficulty in walking, and though things seemed to improve a little, she had to return to the doctor who had operated on her. For the first time she was told that the real trouble was that she had degenerative multiple sclerosis. At least there was the relief of being given a name to what before had been an unknown condition. This helped to get things in perspective for her. It could not be shown whether the M.S. had been caused by the accident. Her condition gradually worsened. She began to need sticks to walk, though increasingly she lost her mobility. She tried various treatments and went regularly for hyperbaric oxygen treatment which inhibited the deterioration, but eventually she was unable to drive even a modified car, and became housebound. It became increasingly difficult to meet the needs of Richard and their daughters.

After five years of suffering with multiple sclerosis, when her husband was working away during the week as a police instructor, she began to notice that not everything seemed quite right with him. She couldn't tell exactly what was wrong, but he seemed to lose his closeness with the Lord, although he was still attending church services.

One night they were talking, when out of the blue Lucy asked him, 'What is troubling you? ... There isn't anyone else, is there?' It was one of those questions that she later said you never know why you have asked. And she never imagined what the real answer would be. There was a pause, then Lucy realised what the problem was. It was a devastating, unexpected, unforgettable moment.

They tried to talk things through, but with no success. Lucy was genuinely shocked that a professing Christian should act in the way that he was doing. Together they sought Christian advice, but Richard made it clear that he did not really want to talk to anyone, and certainly did not want help. It was not just that he was in a deepening relationship with a student policewoman, but he didn't want to stay in a home with a woman whose M.S. was deteriorating and demanding. Very soon, Richard left the church and his physically impaired wife and two daughters. The children were frightened that their mother would leave them too.

After some years of coping in her own home, with a lift being fitted, and then eventually having to live just downstairs, she moved to a Leonard Cheshire Home. Lucy's father had died, but a friend who worked in the Special Branch of her police force as well as the church got behind her and the girls in what was to become a long-term commitment of care. 'But the greatest blessing for me,' said Lucy, 'is knowing that the Lord is with me. When Richard eventually left, I had a great peace from God. At first I thought, "How am I going to sort out everything? What will I do about the finances? What will happen to the house?" Yet I can honestly say that I had such a peace and assurance that the Lord was with me. That was the great truth that sustained me. I can remember thinking afterwards that if I could have Richard back but not have this peace with the Lord, I wouldn't want Richard back. The Lord has been such a comfort to me.

'Of course, I have wondered, "Why?" I don't know the purpose the Lord has in it, but I am confident that He does have a purpose, and that He knows full well what He is doing. I believe God called Richard and me together. God does not make mistakes. I don't know the final outcome, but I at least I know God, and He is in control.

'Spiritually my life is deeper; I have realised that my walk with the Lord is the most important part of my life. Even when I was feeling very hurt and Richard had told me that he didn't love me anymore, I thought of the fact that God sent His only Son to die for me, as He did for Richard. But now Richard has turned round and thrown God's love back in the Lord's face. So how must the Lord feel when He loved Richard so much that He died for Him? It's not just me that's hurting, it is the Lord as well.'

During her 10 years in the Leonard Cheshire Home, Lucy was well cared for. She was always cheerful, praying for, and asking after others. When possible she made it to church, but slowly she lost all her mobility, and eventually the strength to even talk. She loved her daughters, her little grandchildren and church friends. She suffered, but through it all sought to honour the God who loved her. Her funeral was a triumphant occasion, and though Richard was not present, her friends prayed for him, and gave thanks for the challenge and blessing of her life.

CHAPTER 8

TEENAGE TRAGEDY
THE STORY OF PAUL KOBRYN

Are not two sparrows sold for a copper coin? And not one of them falls to the ground apart from your Father's will. But the very hairs of your head are all numbered. Do not fear therefore; you are of more value than many sparrows. (Matthew 10:29–31, NKJV)

'My earliest memories are of being taken away from my mother by the police or social workers. Sometimes the Fire Service had to break down the doors to get me. The social worker had to wrench me from my mother. She was suffering from a severe mental illness at the time, and was unable to look after me,' says Paul Kobryn, as he reflects on his life, which by any standard has not been easy.

Paul was moved to a Children's Home where he was to spend much of his childhood. He made frequent visits home but they were always very traumatic because of his mother's erratic behaviour. Eventually he was made a Ward of Court for his own protection. Inevitably this affected his schooling so he fell behind his classmates. He was unable to concentrate because of his emotional problems, so at the age of nine he was sent to a special school.

By the time Paul was 12 he asked to be fostered by a family. It was a huge step for him for he feared what his mother's reaction would be. She accepted his wishes though, so eventually Paul was introduced to his future foster parents, Ray and Pat, and began to spend weekends with them. 'Already God was working in my situation,' says Paul. Although at the time he didn't know it, Pat and Ray were Christians and had been praying that the Lord would lead them to the right child to foster. At the same time, the Christian head of the Children's Home had been praying for a Christian foster home for him.

'When I was in the Children's Home we were sent to a Bible class,' Paul continues. 'One of the things I was looking forward to when I was fostered was not having to go any more; but to my dismay, on the first Sunday with Ray and Pat, off we went to church! I wasn't at all happy with this, and found it very boring.' Pat and Ray already had two children of their own, but the whole family quickly accepted Paul. He found it strange that their home was so 'open'. Money would be lying around because there was a basic trust and honesty. As a family they shared everything openly, not only their material possessions but also their feelings and problems.

However, over the four years of sharing in family life Paul found it hard to adjust. He says that he was stubborn and had many arguments with his foster parents. He didn't feel they gave him enough time, and when he looked at other children with their 'real' parents, he felt left out and deprived. People he knew, even Christians, had different and varying standards and he found this confusing.

During his first year with his foster parents, Paul debated with Pat and Ray about their Christian faith. He found it difficult to see their point of view on many issues, varying from the creation of the world to the forgiveness of sins. The problems and difficulties in his life seemed to mount and appeared overwhelming. Ultimately Paul became so uneasy and worried about his problems that he decided to turn to God for help. He describes what happened on Sunday, 16 January 1983 at a church service in Alton in Hampshire. He was a teenager. 'It was an unforgettable day. I committed my life to Jesus Christ. My reaction was incredible! I was so excited. I immediately went out to buy a new Bible. I had previously found the Bible had no meaning for me, but after that step of commitment, it came to life. It meant something to me. I began to understand it more and to see how it applied to my everyday life. I started to realise all that Jesus had done for me by His death on the cross. He was taking on Himself the punishment for my sins. Church too became a pleasure, not a duty. I got involved in church services, in United Beach Missions, and something called "Mission Solent", all of which I loved.'

But somehow the initial enthusiasm didn't last. 'I still had my problems because of all the upheavals in my life and lack of a trusting family background. I found it difficult to adjust to my foster family, and found it hard to trust them or the Lord. It was hard to ask the family for anything, even such a simple thing as a packet of crisps. I would just help myself. It would never occur to me to give advance warning of a weekend Scout camp. I didn't mean to hurt the feelings of my foster parents, but I was used to keeping myself to myself, relying on my own company. Gradually things began to change. I became more interested in Scouts and less concerned about Christian things and following God's way for my life.

'Pat and Ray were thinking of moving away, and I was discussing with my social worker the possibility of a flat of my own and a Youth Training Scheme course on child care. I booked into a three-week Scout camp for underprivileged Asian children from the East End of London and ruled out the more Christian activity of beach missions. I was determined to go to camp, and God wasn't going to stop me!'

Paul felt that he himself had been hurt greatly by adults and that children ought to have their rights. His inner rebellion was growing as he started to do things he knew he ought not to do. His spiritual life and the joy he had experienced in Christ were waning.

It was during this period of spiritual decline, whilst on his way to sixth form college that Paul had a terrible accident. He was on his bicycle when he was hit by a car. It was 11 June 1986 on a very wet and dark Wednesday morning. He was cycling on a busy, wide road near the centre of Southampton, preparing to turn right, when a car whose driver, for whatever reason, did not see him and hit him from behind. He was thrown back and then somersaulted forward. His neck was irreparably broken. The driver was eventually fined £65 for driving without due care and attention.

But God had not forsaken Paul. Within minutes four significant people were on the scene of the accident – a nurse, a man who knew his foster mother, a policeman and a Christian friend who was able to pray for the Lord's help in the situation.

Retelling the story, Paul says, 'When I came round in the hospital, I was told that I was paralysed from the shoulders down. I have no recollection of the first traumatic week, but just hazy memories of seeing people's feet when I was upside down on the Stryker frame. Because of the shock my first worries were wondering what had happened to my bike and my clothes.

'Then followed a year in a Spinal Injuries Unit at Stoke Mandeville Hospital. I had three major operations, which were so serious that for a while my life was in jeopardy. I had many queries and feared that, like Job in the Old Testament, God would allow further calamities to befall me. However, John, a Christian physiotherapist at the unit, was a source of enormous support and encouragement to me, and I gradually recovered my strength. When I was transferred to a recovery unit he arranged for me to attend a nearby church, where I received such a warm and loving welcome. Friends wrote and visited, many people prayed, and gradually light began to shine at the end of the tunnel.'

Eventually Paul was able to move to adapted accommodation in a bungalow. He was still in a wheelchair and paralysed as before, but he was able to continue his studies at college, as well as being involved with Young Life, an inter-church youth movement, and the Scouts. The people in each of these groups remained faithful friends to him throughout his treatment. One of the many letters he received was from Joni Eareckson Tada in the USA.[1] Paul found transport a problem, and had to rely on friends for lifts, or wait for transport to be provided by the Unit.

'Through it all, I've grown spiritually and learned to trust God more. He has given me a sense of peace and purpose; I have been able to share my faith with people and in places to which before I would never have had access. I am praying that in the future perhaps God will enable me to help in establishing some sort of ministry for the disabled to help me share the hope and new life which have become so real to me.'

Needless to say, Paul has often wondered why this has happened, but it is not a question that troubles him now. He will tell anyone who asks that the Christian life is not immune from bad circumstances. Hanging in Paul's room is a plaque on which are the words that God does not promise sun without rain, but He does give grace and strength to meet all our needs. Paul has said to many people, 'I accept God's will, even though I don't have any explanations. Frankly, I deserve far worse because of all my sin.'

Of course it is hard when Paul sees other Christians for whom life seems so smooth and easy, but he gladly testifies to the fact that God has drawn much closer to him and means much more since the accident.

Though he has no glib answers, Paul at least tries to be

---

[1] Joni had become paralysed at the age of 17 whilst diving into what proved to be shallow water in the Chesapeake Bay in Maryland. Her writings and aid work called Joni and Friends have been an inspiration to millions around the world. Her autobiography is called *Joni* and has been made into a feature film. See www.joniandfriends.org.

honest. He says that life is hard work now and he doesn't enjoy it like he used to. Everything is a hassle, but he also says that this temporary physical life isn't what is most important. He feels that 'people foolishly rush about doing this and that, not realising that they could die at any moment. Actually what Jesus will want to know is how real our life was; did we know Him, and have we lived for eternity or only for time?'

Paul says, 'If it wasn't for wanting to spread the gospel, and proclaim that "Christ died for our sins according to the Scriptures, and that He was buried and that He rose again on the third day", I would want to go straight to heaven today! But even now, though all this life is a spiritual battle, the Lord stays with me. He speaks so clearly to me through His Word, the Bible. I trust Him for everything – I have no other choice. As God says in Jeremiah 23:23, "[I am] a God near at hand ... And not a God afar off" (NKJV).'

Paul spoke those words when he was in his early 20s, and perhaps they are easy to dismiss. But none of his trust has passed with the years.

CHAPTER 9

A MARRIAGE MADE IN HEAVEN?

THE STORY OF DAVID AND SANDRA HUMPHREYS

The LORD is a refuge for the oppressed, a stronghold in times of trouble. (Psalm 9:9)

Until he took early retirement, David was a policeman in the Staffordshire Police Force. He first met Sandra when he was on the beat in Stafford town centre. Sandra was working at the local Town Clerk's office and was regularly delivering mail to the police station.

Dave had been brought up in the country. His father worked in the timber yard on the local estate. Though he went to a good school he feels he wasted his opportunity to learn, as he spent most of his time playing cricket, representing both his school and his county. And as his father was also caretaker of the local men's club, Dave used to go there and play billiards. He left school at 17 with just one 'O' level – in English Language. He applied to join the Police Cadets without any clear reason for doing so.

After going out with each other for two years, Sandra and Dave were married. At the beginning everything was fine. Sandra was working and they were both earning sufficient money to be able to spend and enjoy themselves. They were carefree, and problem-free.

Problems started though, when their first daughter, Kerry, was born after three years of marriage. At first Dave was a proud and doting father, but that didn't last. By the time their second daughter, Joanne, arrived three years later, Dave was spending a lot of time away from home. In the summer he played cricket, which involved socialising and drinking after the matches. In the winter he would go out playing cribbage and darts, but again, they both involved a lot of drinking.

Sandra suffered from post-natal depression after the birth of Joanne. Now they lacked money as Sandra was no longer working, and there were two little ones to feed and care for. Dave did not cope with the depression, which was triggering a vicious circle of problems. The more depressed Sandra became, the more Dave went out, and the more he was out, the more depressed she became.

The only person Sandra felt she could talk to was a friend who was also suffering from depression. This merely served to worsen her depressed state rather than solving any problems.

Sandra had been brought up without a father. When she was suffering from depression her doctor said to her that he felt she was perhaps being unfair to Dave because she was expecting him to be both a father and a husband to her. The doctor didn't feel that Dave was able to do that.

On the other hand, throughout all the difficulties Dave would never admit that he had a problem. He had, of course, seen other people with problems. Anyone who was drinking as regularly and as much as he was has a problem, but Dave did not feel addicted to alcohol. He would always say that he was not going out for a drink, but just to enjoy the company.

When Kerry was five, Sandra's sister-in-law, who was Kerry's godmother, asked if Kerry could go to Sunday school. Her sister-in-law was a Christian and took very seriously the vows she had made at Kerry's christening. She asked if Sandra would take Kerry to Sunday school at the local Baptist church which was just down the road from where they lived. Sandra agreed, and at first would take Kerry then just leave her at the Sunday school before going straight back home. After a few weeks, the minister's wife asked if she would stay for the service. She did, and enjoyed it immensely. She was impressed with the friendliness of the people who were there, and looked forward to the services. But she was still struggling with depression, and was on anti-depressant tablets. Dave wasn't bothered about her going to church as long as it didn't affect him. Gradually she progressed from going once a month to going every week.

Some time later, Sandra and a friend went to a nightclub. Surprisingly, in the middle of the concert, one of the singers interrupted his performance by telling his story as to how he had become a Christian. Then he sang a couple of Christian songs. One was called, 'Such is the mystery', and was about all the free things that God gives in creation to everybody. At the end the singer stood, arms outstretched in the shape of a cross with a red spotlight on him. It really affected Sandra, as she thought that if this person could stand up in a nightclub and say what Jesus had done for him, with people heavily drinking and smooching all around him, she knew that it must mean something that is real.

Later, she spoke to her brother, who was a Christian. Over the years he had spent a lot of time with Sandra and the girls, particularly on Sundays. They would sit in the house and talk. Sandra wanted to know what made someone a Christian, and was realising that she wanted to become one. She says, 'I felt at that stage that I really wanted to know Jesus as my Saviour. It had made such a difference in others, and in the singer I heard. He could actually stand up publicly in difficult places and tell his story, so it clearly meant such a lot to him. I wanted that for myself.

'My brother explained the gospel to me and said that I needed to pray and repent of my sins. Jesus had died, paying for my sins so that I could be forgiven. I had to ask Jesus into my life, which I did. But I don't think anything dramatic happened at that stage, and I didn't really feel any different, except that I started to read my Bible, and I started to pray day by day. I was aware of God and thought about Him an awful lot.'

However, the real turning point came some months later. Sandra tells her story:

'Dave had been playing in an all-day cricket match. He went out quite early in the morning and he didn't arrive home until the early hours of the following morning. When he came into the bedroom he was obviously drunk, and when I spoke to him, it became apparent that he didn't even know where he was, and certainly couldn't remember driving home.

'He had been drunk on occasions before but he had never actually driven the car in that state. He didn't even know how he had got home, and that made me very angry. I said it was totally irresponsible to be driving a car in that condition. He could have killed someone. I could not stand drinking, and every time he came in smelling of beer it made me angry; but this really affected me quite badly. We ended up having a blazing row. We had had rows before, hundreds of them. But during this row he hit me, which he had never done before. It was quite violent in that I actually landed on the floor and hit my head. By this time Kerry and Joanne were both awake and the three of us were crying. I got them into bed with me and pleaded with Dave to go and sleep in one of the girls' beds and to leave us alone. He ranted and raved a bit and kept storming round the bed and shouting things at me about how I was mad and needed to be put in a mental home.

'Things were getting worse and I cried out to God. I prayed, "God, if you are there, please help me now … I need your help now." Suddenly a tremendous sense of peace came over me and I stopped crying, became quite rational and just talked to Dave, so that he went out and got into one of the girls' beds. Then I put my arms around the girls and they stopped crying and we went to sleep. It was something I had never been able to do before. When we had had rows previously, I would lie awake for most of the night very upset and sometimes very angry as well. But this time I felt this wonderful peace and knew that Jesus really was in my life. I felt absolutely marvellous the next day. I had no effects at all from the bump on my head or anything else. I actually went and told the minister's wife and my brother about what had happened. They were both as convinced as I was that the Lord had indeed come into my life.'

At first Sandra felt that their marriage was over. She did not feel she had any love left for Dave. They seemed to want totally different things out of life. She believed that things had become so bad between them that nothing could make any difference. She shared this with the minister's wife who responded to Sandra saying, 'Oh no, I am sure the Lord does not want you to leave Dave. I know it is going to be difficult, but we will meet together and we'll pray for him and we will see what happens.' Gradually, over the times of prayer that they had when they met, Sandra became convinced that God would 'save' Dave – that he too would trust God for salvation – but secretly she thought it would be when Dave was a lot older.

Dave was deeply sceptical about Christians and very anti-Christian in his world view. Sandra would 'drop' little things about God into their everyday conversations. Dave could not help but see a huge difference in her. There was less aggravation and argument. Her attitude to him and those around her was different, and clearly she had a love for the Lord that was increasingly radiating through her.

Eventually Dave came to the point where he was not happy in himself. He did not want to merely see a change in Sandra, but he wanted to experience it for himself as well. He says, 'I saw more contentment in her life and I was not contented. I was attracted to it to such an extent that even though in my own heart I would have wanted to resist it, I felt I had to respond to God's claim on my life. I went to church and I was quite impressed. I do not remember anything of what I now know as "the gospel" but I can remember the friendliness of the people there. I can remember singing hymns that I had not sung before that seemed to be a happier sort of hymn than I had experienced in church as a child. In 1 Peter 3 in the Bible we read about wives making an impression on their husbands, not by their appearance but by the way they are, and that was exactly what was impressing me. At that time I had not considered myself as a sinner in need of forgiveness, but I saw something that I thought would make me happier, and it was something I wanted to pursue.'

It was about 12 months after Sandra had been converted that Dave himself trusted Christ as Lord and Saviour. 'I knew enough to realise that I had to ask Jesus into my life. I can remember walking along the road and being upset about my situation, and I can remember just simply asking Jesus to come into my life, and that was it. I came home and told Sandra what I had done,' Dave recalls. He had put his trust in the crucified, risen Christ.

It made an immediate difference, but there were difficulties to overcome because the situation within the family was still the same. Dave felt challenged about how he was using his life and money. He stopped smoking, as much for health reasons as for anything else, but as soon as he stopped he found that he had no desire to smoke again. Some Christian friends talked to him about drink. They didn't say he shouldn't go out for a drink, but asked if he really felt that the pub was where he ought to be. They asked whether he would rather spend his time with the people in the pub or with his own family. From that time on he never went back to the pub on a Friday night.

The next year Dave and Sandra were baptised by full immersion during a church service. Dave says, 'As I look back, and perhaps I did not realise it then, the Lord did not only save me, He saved our marriage, because I am sure that if I had not been saved we would not be married now. I would have lost my wife and my family. That would have all gone and been destroyed. I am convinced of that.

'One of the first tests of our faith was that we prayed about having another child and felt it was right to do that. Sandra became pregnant very quickly and had a trouble-free pregnancy until the 15th week when she miscarried. We were devastated by it and could not understand why God had let it happen when it was the baby we had prayed for.'

'But there again,' says Sandra, 'God met me in a very special way when I had the miscarriage. Although we might not know the reasons for these things happening, there is a reason for it, and I believe the Lord has enabled me to talk with other people I have since met who have had miscarriages. He blessed us with Gemma the following year and she has been a very special joy to all of us. We had two daughters during the non-Christian part of our marriage and it was nice to have a daughter within a Christian marriage; we felt that was quite important. We thank God that His blessing has been upon us. As well, our three daughters are Christians and have been saved the pain and misery that we brought upon ourselves.'

Both Dave and Sandra are involved in their local church, which they thoroughly enjoy. Do they ever argue now? With a mischievous smile on his face, Dave replies, 'Oh, no, never! Never let the sun go down on your anger! The sun has gone down on my anger on a number of occasions, but when we have differences of opinion we are able to deal with them, and we know that the Lord is in the midst of our family. We know that He is active in our lives; we know He is there, and when irritations arise we are able to overcome our difficulties by bringing them to God in prayer.'

CHAPTER 10

LIVING IN A SILENT WORLD

THE STORY OF JOHN HILL

In that day the deaf shall hear the words of the book,
And the eyes of the blind shall see out of obscurity and
out of darkness. (Isaiah 29:18, NKJV)

I have debated in my mind whether it is more difficult to be born totally blind or completely deaf. To never understand the concepts of colour and shade, or not be able to remember sights and admire beauty is a huge handicap. However, as someone who loves sound, conversation, discussion and music, to be deaf would be overwhelmingly difficult.

John was born in the historic county town of Dorchester in Dorset in 1962, the youngest of three children. His early years were spent in the picture-postcard village of Cerne Abbas, where his father was the gardener for Lord and Lady Digby. Their extensive grounds required the service of a full-time gardener, and John's father redesigned the already beautiful gardens. As a family, they lived in a tied cottage next to the manor house where the Digbys lived and entertained many guests. Soon after John's birth, the Hill family moved to Cricket St. Thomas in Somerset.

John has a few memories of his early childhood. His parents and two older sisters were incredibly poor, and John tells of one particularly cold winter where thick snow lay on the ground for weeks, with very little food to go round the whole family. Life was difficult, and typically his mother always gave most to the rest of the family leaving little for herself. John's grandparents and uncle were a great help by giving the family food and clothing, but times were very tough.

His parents, at that time, were not professing Christians, though his grandfather was a great lover of the Bible, reading and studying it daily. One imagines that he prayed for his grandchildren and their particular needs. John's oldest sister, Dorothy, who was 12 years his senior, attended grammar schools in Dorchester, Ilminster and later in Teignmouth, before becoming a nurse, later marrying, having children and writing some best-selling books. However, Barbara, four years older than John, had Down's syndrome. Needless to say, this created its own challenges: such as the time when Barbara, aged only seven or eight, had been lost, only to be eventually found in a dishevelled state in the rubbish bin.

John was still very young when his sister Dorothy accidentally dropped a tea tray on the floor, but noticed that John did not jump at the noise. It was the first indication that John was deaf. As a child, John was taken to the doctor and given two hearing aids but, being totally deaf, they were of no help! Of course, because he has never been able to hear, John is mute. Physiologically John would be able to speak, but has never heard any sounds enabling him to learn speech. John actually has a rare condition – Klippel-Feil[2] syndrome. As a young child his arms remained by his side without movement. He couldn't catch a ball or ring a bell, his hands just hung down. He couldn't hold the ropes on a swing, and he never had the ability to suck his thumb! His father patiently tried to bring mobility to his arms. But John clearly remembers how when he was still very young suddenly his brain 'woke up' so that he could move his arms. He had repeated visits to hospital for X-rays on his neck.

At the age of just three-and-a-half, John was sent away to Exeter School for the Deaf to board during the weekdays. He had a good friend who also was deaf, and their mothers talked and looked for ways to help their sons. However, John's parents had little choice except to allow him to board in Exeter where there were 50 to 60 other children, boys and girls, some partially and others totally deaf. But it was tough being away from home and parents at such a young age. They had a school uniform, which the school provided as his parents couldn't afford to buy one for him. Neither could his parents afford the little treats that other children enjoyed. John stayed there until it was time to leave full-time education. His world revolved around the activities of the school. He recalls that the kitchens and toilet facilities were not great so there were issues with food poisoning and sicknesses

---

[2] Klippel-Feil syndrome is a rare bone disorder characterised by abnormal joining of two or more spinal bones in the neck.

with the children. At the age of five, he had breathing difficulties and was rushed to hospital.

To be near the school the family moved again, living at the top of a steep hill – Break Neck Hill in Teignmouth, close to the place where actress Vivien Leigh met her first husband. The family would huddle around the Rayburn to keep warm in the cold winter months.

Bizarrely, the children had to sit on their hands, because the educational thinking at that time was to not learn sign language but lip-reading. John remembers one girl who also had difficulty with her sight and so could never master lip-reading and consequently she was regarded as a failure.

Next to the school was St. Leonard's Church, an active and thriving church. Each Friday a team from the church would visit the school and share Bible stories. John remembers going in a long line with school cap and coat, hand in hand with another pupil to visit the church. They all sat down looking at the front of the church. Sadly though, John did not understand much of what was being taught. But he does remember that these visits were his first introduction to Bible characters such as Mary, Joseph and the baby Jesus. As he was growing up, this continued, but he still had very little understanding of Christianity.

Dorothy had become a Christian at the age of 16 when John was just four. She had gone on a coach trip from Ilminster to hear Dr. Billy Graham, the American evangelist, who was preaching in Earls Court in London. She remembers not only hearing the gospel being preached that night, but also Ethel Waters singing, 'His eye is on the sparrow'. The next night in Illminster she told her youth leader that she wanted to become a Christian, and prayed asking Jesus to become her Lord and Saviour. She started to volunteer in the summer holidays to work with United Beach Missions who run family activities in holiday centres throughout Europe. Dorothy took John to the missions in Paignton in Devon. John was six or seven years old. They would go by train and spend the morning and afternoon there, then their father would pick them up at the end of the day. The mission would organise games and activities as well as singing Christian songs and teaching Bible stories.

As they sang, Dorothy would do actions to go along with the words, so John became familiar with children's songs such as:

Wide, wide as the ocean
High as the heavens above
Deep, deep as the deepest sea
Is my Saviour's love.
I, though so unworthy,
Still am a child of His care,
For His word teaches me
That His love reaches me ...
Everywhere.

Without ever hearing words, it was hard for John to understand all that was being taught, but his heart was drawn to God. It was probably at this time that John first found himself putting his trust in Jesus, but his understanding was limited. At school he found a big Bible in the library and took it to his room trying to read and understand it. None of the other pupils seemed to be interested in the Bible, but a lady who had been a teacher at the school used to visit and helped him with the Bible stories. At the time he didn't understand concepts such as 'Jesus, the Lamb of God' or why the blood of Jesus seemed so important.

At the end of his street in Teignmouth was a Gospel Hall. John and a hearing friend used to play together, and on Sundays they would go to the afternoon services of the little church. His parents had to look after Barbara, but faithfully the boys went and watched the services. People were very friendly, but once again John could not understand the service.

A few months before he was 16, John saw someone signing privately to a small group. It was all new to him and his friends at school. He still was not permitted to sign, but it was bewildering to him as to why this had been kept from him. Along with a friend and with great difficulty, he began to slowly learn sign language. To this day, John wonders why a strange educational theory should have been permitted to have such influence to the detriment of hundreds of young, disadvantaged people.

On leaving school, he was presented with a Bible. John tried to read, but he couldn't understand. He would see people talking, but what was going on was beyond his reach. He tried to find work but there were too many obstacles for employers to overcome. He kept going to find jobs, but without success. It was tough living at home with few who could communicate with him, and John found himself lonely and becoming depressed. He would walk alone for hours.

When John was 25 his father died. Again, John was to 'hear' the gospel signed to him at his father's funeral, but John's spirit was low. A month later there were twists and turns in his life, which left John feeling angry and frustrated with his lot. He was getting thinner, and life seemed to have no meaning for him.

Very early one morning, he was walking alone along the coastal path. John saw the sun rising, creating a path of light across the water. The way the light was configured, it seemed to him that at the end of the pathway there was Jesus on the cross. He knows it was not reality, but the faraway shape was to remind him of the love of Jesus for him. It was if God was saying, 'Hold on: hold on to Me, and I will hold on to you.' To a deaf person, the visual impact was incredibly helpful. Before this he feared that he was not ready to die and life was meaningless, but now he knew that God had him in His grip.

At the same time his sister Dorothy, who lived in Yorkshire, helped to arrange a place for John to study carpentry at Doncaster College for the Deaf. She also leaned sign language which enabled them to have more normal conversations and develop deeper family ties. John also linked up with an inter-denominational youth group called Young Life. Two of the leaders of the group, Robert and Simon, showed particular care for John. They taught him the meaning of words like 'belief' and 'trust', explaining how God cares for him; how Jesus died on the cross for John's sin; how He rose from the dead, as well as John's need to ask God for forgiveness and new life in Jesus. Bit by bit, John began to understand more. His understanding of English was built on nouns and verbs, there was no grammar, so reading was always going to be difficult for him. With a very gradual but growing understanding about God, he was trusting in God. He knew spiritual battles of being pulled towards and away from God, but his faith and spiritual awareness were growing.

After qualifying in carpentry at Doncaster, John moved to Leeds, where he still lives. He qualified for a council flat and started work as a caretaker/cleaner for the N.H.S. He has worked in four different health centres. He has regularly received letters from his bosses commending his high standard of work. For over 20 years he has never been late, nor missed a day's work. His flat is filled with items of interest due to his many hobbies. He loves having the opportunity to visit the seaside to look for fossils and coloured stones, so has an interesting collection, as well as a vast array of unusual coins, stamps and other items. If he had not been deaf, John would have wanted to join the Royal Navy, possibly as a submariner. He has several books about ships, which have always fascinated him. When he was a young teenager, his father and he saved to buy a good-quality telescope, so John has always enjoyed looking at stars. He has been able to travel to visit relatives in South America and New Zealand, collecting souvenirs and hundreds of photos of his visits. His trust in God has enabled him to be content, though he is aware that there are many things that his deafness prohibits him from doing. He likes to play the piano, though he cannot hear the music at all, but it is part of his worship to God.

John started attending an evangelical church in Harrogate, which tries to have signers for each evening service, as well as running a Fellowship for the Deaf each month. This ministry, until recently led by Marianne, who was the Vice-Principal of a school for the deaf and blind, was a significant help to John, who began to grow in his understanding of the Bible, and of God's purposes for him. He has a very strong sense of right and wrong. In 1996 John felt very sure about his faith, and asked to be baptised by full immersion as an outward sign that he was a Christian believer. The pastor of his church, who had been very kind to him, baptised him, and an evangelist preached the gospel, including telling the story of John and how he came to faith in Jesus. The church was packed with friends whom he had met at different stages of his life.

There are many things John would still struggle to understand, but he is very certain of the God who loved him and came into the world to save him. Many are not able to cope with someone who is deaf and struggles to communicate. But John is sure that he is forgiven and when he meets God, he will be accepted because of all that Jesus has done for him. As he says using British Sign Language, 'In my heart, I know my sins are forgiven. I can't explain everything, and there are lots of things I don't know. It is very hard, because there is so much that is difficult and hard to understand, but I trust Jesus. I dream of what things will be like after I die!'

CHAPTER 11

MURDER IN THE FRONT YARD
THE STORY OF BERYL QUIGLEY

*For I am persuaded that neither death nor life, nor
angels nor principalities nor powers, nor things present
nor things to come, nor height nor depth, nor any other
created thing, shall be able to separate us from the
love of God which is in Christ Jesus our Lord.*
(Romans 8:38–39, NKJV)

'I was privileged to be brought up in a home where we had
the habit of going to church. At the age of nine, as the result
of a children's mission which was held at our church, I knew in
my young heart that I was hearing something I wanted to know
more about, and I made a commitment to Jesus Christ.' So said
Beryl McConnell, widow of the Deputy Governor of the Maze
Prison who was murdered by terrorists during 'the troubles' in
Northern Ireland. 'After the commitment I did not feel much

different, but there was always the desire to know more about Jesus.' As a child she attended Sunday school. Later she was to become a Sunday school teacher in an attempt to give the children something she had received.

When she was 17, understanding more about the Christian message, who Jesus was and what He had done for her, she recommitted her life to Jesus in a more meaningful way. She understood more about the need to repent and receive forgiveness from the Christ who had lived, died and risen from the dead. She began to understand more of the love of God and the sacrifice that He had made through the death of the Lord Jesus. The fact that Jesus had died for her, 'a pathetic sort of creature' (as she puts it) made her believe that she could not go through life without committing herself to this God.

Beryl did not marry early in life. She wanted to be sure she was marrying the right man, and he just didn't turn up until, through a complicated arrangement, Beryl was introduced to Bill. 'I think it is lovely if you can meet somebody and fall in love and get married when you are young, but I didn't meet "Mr. Right". A friend of mine who met Bill through her work had said to me, "I know somebody who would suit you," so I immediately asked, "Where is this guy?" At that stage he was working in Magilligan Prison, so it was some months before she arranged a supper party and, unknown to me, invited Bill as well as me. During the evening, I noticed that when he was talking there was a depth to him, and he was genuinely interested in people. He seemed to have a fair amount of knowledge about a number of subjects. It also struck me that he had thought through a number of things and was very clear in his own mind where he stood on certain issues. I thought, "Here's a guy who really knows where he is going.' It was his strength of character that really appealed to Beryl.

Bill had been brought up in a Christian home in Holywood just near to Belfast. Whilst at school he joined the Christian group that met regularly, and began to realise that Christianity is not something reserved for Sundays only. He became aware of what God was doing in the lives of his school friends. It was their influence which really led him to make a commitment to the Lord Jesus Christ when he was still at school.

They were married in 1979 and their marriage lasted a fortnight short of five years. They had a little girl who went on to become a doctor. She was three when her father was murdered.

It was in 1983 when 38 prisoners broke out of the notorious Maze Prison that the final chapter in the life of Bill McConnell began. There was a huge outcry following the breakout, so that Sir James Hennessy and a team of investigators were despatched to enquire how the escape could have happened. Their report, which was published in January 1984, made certain points about which the Governor and his staff were deeply unhappy. Therefore it was decided, though it had never been done before, that a public reply would have to be made. Bill McConnell, who had responsibility for allocating work to resentful prisoners, offered to be the spokesperson and became a focal point for both the local and national media. Interviews were arranged. One local radio station went to their home in the leafy suburb of East Belfast to make a taped recording to be broadcast on 3 February. An ITV crew had also gone from England to the McConnells' house. While the equipment, cameras, microphones and backdrop were being set up in their home, Bill and Beryl talked very briefly.

There was a lot going on: phones were ringing, people were moving around and chattering, but the couple talked about where this could lead. Beryl said, 'You know, Bill, you could lose your job. You could end up in prison if you say too much. You could be breaking the Official Secrets Act and end up in your own prison.' Then she added, 'It could bring about your death.' To this day Beryl doesn't know why she said it, but she did feel it was a possibility. Paramilitaries had already killed 22 prison officers during the Troubles, and to draw attention to oneself like that was clearly dangerous. They didn't talk any more about it, but they did commit the situation to the Lord in prayer, saying that whatever was in the future was in God's hands and they would rest secure in Him.

Unknown to Beryl, the next morning, after the radio interviews had been done and the television interview recorded, Bill went into his work office and wrote a letter. During the 30 years of conflict in Northern Ireland it was not unusual for people there to write a testamentary letter because they were doing a job that entailed a certain amount of danger. Usually the letters would ask for certain hymns to be sung at the funeral as well as making other funeral arrangements. Bill did that but also left his Christian testimony, which was actually printed after his murder in a number of national newspapers.

The letter said that he didn't know who may want to kill him, but that whoever it was, he was sorry for them. It said:

You will be gathered today asking questions which only

a full investigation of the facts will reveal. Clearly, in attempting that process to continue, someone has decided that I should play no further part in the proceedings. I feel sorry for them, and can only pray that their part in the story will one day be revealed.

My wife, Beryl, has been supportive of all I have done. I would commend her and Gail to your keeping and prayers.

Finally, let no one be alarmed as to my eternal security. In March 1966 I committed my life, talents, work and actions to Almighty God in sure and certain knowledge that however slight my hold upon Him may have been during my years at school, university and the prison service, His promises are sure, and His hold on me complete.

Nothing can separate me from the love of God in Christ Jesus our Lord. [3]

He had given the letter, in a sealed envelope, to one of his Christian colleagues in the prison.

At the time some felt that Bill may have been too casual about his personal security. He left his car outside the house instead of in the garage. He often did not even lock it. He had been issued with a gun and trained to use it, but did not carry it. He had been measured for a flak jacket. He brought it home where it was put

---

[3] *The Times*, 9 March 1984

in the cloakroom to gather dust. On one occasion Beryl had said, 'You are going to have to be more careful because there could be a car bomb one morning.'

He replied saying, 'Look, sit down while I speak to you. I have committed my life to the Lord and I am not going to die one second before the Lord wants me to go to heaven. I don't know how I am going to die or when I am going to die. If it means I am going to die at the end of a bullet fired by a terrorist gunman, it is the way the Lord has it and I am happy with that.'

The day of Bill's murder began as a very ordinary day in their lives. It was a Tuesday morning, 6 March 1984. Bill was having breakfast, little Gail was chattering, and Beryl went out of the house and cleaned the windows of the car so he could jump into it and head off to work, as he always seemed to leave late. She helped Bill on with his coat. They had their usual hugs and kisses. 'Because,' as Beryl explains, 'each time he left home, either to go to work or church, or a Scout meeting, we always said our goodbyes as if it might be the last time. One never knows when death can strike – you don't have to be old or infirm; death can come very quickly, to young and old alike.' They then went out to the car, which was parked at the front of the house. Beryl noticed things happening around the house directly across the road from them, things that were not normal.

An elderly couple lived opposite them. They were not usually out and about at 8.15 in the morning, but Beryl noticed that their silver Metro was in the drive, not in the garage, and it was facing towards the street instead of away from it as it usually would have been. She thought something was wrong. Then she saw a couple of young men coming out of the drive, and she started trying to put answers to what was happening. 'What were these people doing? They were not bin men – no, it is not bin day.' Suddenly she realised, as they started to come across the road towards their gate, that they were in fact carrying guns and were preparing to fire them. Seeing that Bill was just about to be shot, she shouted a warning to him. He turned, saw them, then spun round in an attempt to avoid being shot. They were only a matter of three or four yards from him whey they opened fire. Bill received a number of bullets in his head and chest and fell dead. He probably died instantly. He died in a pool of blood while 'the moisture of our last kiss was still on my lips,' says Beryl. The gun was an automatic pistol and the bullets just flew into his body. Gail was there and saw what happened. When the bangs started she was frightened and cried and screamed, then ran into the house. She didn't actually see her father and the mess that was around his body. The attack was over in seconds.

With bullets flying all around, and two gunmen, Beryl was not sure whether she was going to be killed or not. Quickly, though, the gunmen left Bill dead on the ground and made their getaway. Beryl realised that it was safe to get up from her crouching position beside Bill's red Vauxhall Cavalier. She could see that Bill was dead, and immediately thought, 'Well, he is in the presence of God at last.' Then as she looked at his body, she says, 'I felt it was almost like clothing that we put on, it was the body in which God had placed his soul, and that soul had gone to be with God in heaven.'

Reflecting on what happened Beryl later said, 'Nobody really knows how they are going to react when something dramatic happens. I must say, I felt calm, I didn't dissolve into tears. In fact, I can honestly say that I never had the feeling that I had to sit down and weep bitter tears. It really did feel that God was with me. And Bill's family, who are Christians, felt that strength because we were not bitter; we were not sad. There was a peace. You know people quote the Bible and speak about this peace beyond human understanding, and that is what we experienced. It must have come from God; where else could it have come from? It was there; it kept me going; it allowed me to speak to people, and in fact my heart went out to other people who probably felt Bill's loss almost more than I did. I had been present at his death and had come to terms with it. But his old friends were coming to the house and they just couldn't take it in. I was actually finding myself trying to comfort them."

Her faith as a little girl aged nine, and rededication at the age of 17 proved real and valuable at this testing time in terrible circumstances. In fact she would say that her faith became stronger as she found that God gave her the strength to get through those difficult days. Through every stage afterwards her faith remained vibrant and God proved to be the source of her strength. She had to look after her young daughter, and in some ways had to be supportive of her husband's parents who had lost their son, as well as his sisters who were bereft of their brother.

One of the men involved in Bill's murder had been a flight lieutenant and RAF pilot then a civil servant for 27 years. Embittered by his lack of promotion he said that his involvement as an unsworn member of the IRA 'was my way of getting revenge on society'. In sentencing him, the judge said, 'How a man of your intelligence, education, background and age [he was 64] could descend into the pits of such murderous intrigue and violence, to join men capable of gunning down a fellow countryman in front of his wife and three-year-old daughter is almost beyond comprehension.'

Another of the convicted killers was given an early release from prison under the terms of the Good Friday Agreement. But Beryl has repeatedly said that none of the family has ever said a bitter word about the people involved. She quickly realised that for her to be able to sleep at night, to be at peace with herself and cope with the new situation she had to be willing to show forgiveness to the murderers. 'We, in fact, have been praying from the time of Bill's death that the people would in some way come to know of the saving grace that God gives. Our prayer has been that God would one day, very soon, speak to them, and that they will come to know the love of Christ and commit their lives to Him. If that happened I would probably be one of the first in the queue to shake hands with them as fellow brothers in the Lord. I know that Bill would be delighted to see them in heaven one day. If it takes Bill's murder to bring these people to the Lord, Bill's murder will have been well and truly worth every second of the loneliness and pain we have suffered.'

A few months before his death, Bill McConnell wrote an article for a church magazine. In it he said, 'The death of an individual at the hands of a murderer, though a tragic event, cannot be considered the ultimate tragedy. We must trust God's sovereignty in these things and thank Him for the life that has passed into eternity.'

Bill's funeral service was to be an act of praising God, not just for Bill's life, but for the fact that he had been saved through the death and resurrection of Jesus Christ. As Gail grew up, the pain and loneliness grew 'bigger and deeper and wider. It was like an awful wound that was constantly being prised open.' But Beryl also began to feel pity for her husband's incarcerated murderers, saying, 'What a worthless way to spend your life. What a total waste of time, and all because hatred and bitterness overcame somebody to such an extent that they carried out a murder.'

Beryl was to remarry, this time to the director of a cancer charity. She acquired three stepsons and found happiness again. Gail 'is miraculously well adjusted,' and does not remember her father's murder. Beryl is sure that one day she will see God's face: 'It must be tremendous to enter into heaven and see at last the face of God and to see Jesus beside Him. It is very exciting to know that that is at the end of our earthly life.'

CHAPTER 12

'I HAVE A FRIEND'
THE STORY OF DAVID JOHNSTONE

*If we confess our sins, [God] is faithful and just
and will forgive us our sins and purify us from all
unrighteousness. (1 John 1:9)*

Born on 4 August 1996, David Johnstone was a healthy, active, outgoing boy who loved sport, especially football, playing for the local football team, Clevedon Town for five years. Football was his great passion in life; his favourite team was Arsenal. He loved being with people, was a friend to many, very popular, sociable and eager to please. He was always active, both in and out of school. He loved going to church with his parents and sister Hannah.

In the summer of 2005 the Johnstone family were in St. Ives in Cornwall, supporting the beach mission[4] being held on Porthminster beach. For decades, as well as organising games

---

and fun activities, the Beach Teams have told Bible stories, sung songs, helped children and families learn about Jesus and understand how He can become their Friend and Saviour. David had heard people say they didn't remember when they actually became Christians, so his young mind thought that he would put his trust in Christ on his eighth birthday, then he would not forget it! He asked Jesus to forgive him and live in his life as his Lord and Saviour.

In September 2006 David complained of a headache. His parents thought it was probably due to lack of sleep but it continued to trouble him. He felt unwell and later started vomiting.

His condition continued to deteriorate. Everything pointed to a typical viral infection, but he became increasingly confused, drifting in and out of consciousness. Further tests at a Neurological Hospital in Bristol followed and a tumour of the brain was diagnosed, necessitating emergency surgery. Intensive chemotherapy reduced the size of the tumour, but he needed seven hours of surgery to remove it. His parents, Andrew and Jane, thought his life was in danger. David himself was very frightened, thinking it was the last time he'd ever see his home and friends. The surgery was successful and after the operation he could not stop talking, telling everyone how God had brought him through.

However, during radiotherapy to his head and just after surgery, further cancerous cells were detected in his spine. In the months that followed, David experienced traumatic radiotherapy and chemotherapy which helped to control the disease but stray cells still remained. In August 2007 the consultants decided on a course of a very high dose of chemotherapy involving stem cell replacement and a month's stay in an isolation unit, taking him to the brink of death and back.

During this time, David had been thinking deeply. Everything that had seemed important to him had been taken away. Even football had lost significance. He knew that God had helped him but began to wonder why God had allowed him to become ill in the first place. He needed to make sure he was in a right relationship with God and asked lots of questions, trying to think things through. Hours of discussions took place with friends and family. He went through three months of turmoil until he came to have absolute assurance that he was God's child, and had been forgiven all the wrong in his young life. He wanted to know he was going to heaven when he died.

His mother wrote out a verse from the Bible for him: 'If we confess our sins, [God] is faithful and just and will forgive us our sins and purify us from all unrighteousness' (1 John 1:9). David reminded himself of that promise many times. A moment came when he realised he could do nothing to make himself right with God, and trusted Jesus to forgive him and live in his life. He was sure he was definitely a Christian, knowing he would never go to hell, but to heaven. Jesus had paid for his sins on the cross and welcomed David as his friend.

David said that even though he loved his family, friends and football, it was more important to him that everything was settled between him and God than that he was healed of cancer. Through his illness David realised he had definitely become a real Christian. The simple trust that he had as a child had matured somewhat to become a deep confident faith, though he was only 11 years old.

On Friday, 28 December 2007, after an MRI scan, the family met with the consultant who said they were losing the battle as the cancer was becoming increasingly aggressive. David's body had taken a battering over 15 months.

'Am I going to die?' David asked.

The consultant replied directly to David, 'Yes, I think you are.'

David, looking at him, said, 'Do you know, I am not afraid because I have a Friend and His name is Jesus, and He died for my sin. I know I am going to heaven.'

The consultant put his hand on David's head and said, 'You know, David, you are a very brave boy. I'm a Christian too. God will help you. Jesus has died and come back to life. He will take you to heaven and will also help your mum and dad.' The nurse, sitting there, just cried.

David wanted his friends to know about Jesus. At church on the last Sunday of 2007, after a special time of testimonies to God's goodness throughout the year, David stood up to say, 'I want to thank you all for your support and prayers for me and my family.'

Early in 2008 a 'Dream Ticket Treat' was arranged for David by the Starlight Trust[5] which fulfils dreams for seriously and terminally ill children. He went to London with his parents and sister to complete his Starlight wish and see *Joseph and his Technicolour Dreamcoat* at the Adelphi Theatre, as well as going on a two-hour tour of the city in a stretch limo. In his last few weeks he managed to pack in much else besides, including going

---

[5] www.starlight.org.uk

with his cousins to see Arsenal play, various friend reunions, a visit to the BBC *Casualty* film set in Bristol and a church holiday in Wales for five days during half term. For David, friends and family were always the most important part of his life.

The children's charity CLIC Sargent[6] was extremely caring to David and his family. At the end of February, he was admitted to the Children's Hospice South West, Charlton Farm,[7] where he died peacefully early on 7 March. Now he is with his greatest Friend and free from suffering forever. The Bible assures us, 'God himself will be with them and … There will be no more death or mourning or crying or pain' (Revelation 21:3–4).

---

[6] www.clicsargent.org.uk
[7] www.chsw.org.uk

CHAPTER 13

FAMILY HANDICAPS
THE STORY OF PHILIP AND CATHERINE CAMPBELL

When you pass through the waters, I will be with you; And through the rivers, they shall not overflow you. When you walk through the fire, you shall not be burned, Nor shall the flame scorch you. For I am the LORD your God... (Isaiah 43:2–3, NKJV)

'Mr. and Mrs. Campbell, we are very sorry but your little daughter will never be normal. She is very severely handicapped. Did you not realise that?'

It is hard to imagine how Philip and Catherine felt that day, sitting facing the paediatrician when their daughter Cheryl was only seven months old. It seemed as though the bottom had dropped out of their world. Everything until then had been fine. Catherine was a qualified nurse and midwife, and Philip at that time was a full-time evangelist leading missions throughout the U.K. They had a very happy, strong marriage. They prayed together about every situation. In fact, during the pregnancy preceding the birth of Cheryl, Philip and Catherine prayed daily that their child would be God's child, knowing and loving Jesus as Saviour. Yet here they were sitting in a consultant's surgery having all their dreams and hopes for that child shattered.

Cheryl, born in August 1979, was their first child and the first grandchild in both families. At first they could not believe what they were hearing. Looking back they would say that, despite the initial shock, they were in the centre of God's will – 'Everything that comes to us is Father-filtered' is a quotation Catherine loves to share. Their world had not come to an end as they had first feared. But that realisation did not come easily.

Catherine, who is a now an accomplished author of several best-selling books as well as an international speaker at women's conferences, shares her early feelings: 'I went to the physiotherapist and worked with Cheryl every day. Godly people laid hands on her and prayed for her. But it didn't make any noticeable difference and I started to shut God out.

'I remember going to a monthly Bible study and hearing about the way we build walls around ourselves and exclude God. I just broke down and cried. I realised that God couldn't help me until I had taken down the walls that I had built round myself. I prayed to God, saying, "I need you and want you to help me." The peace that came into the room was as if it was flooded. I was still hurting. Cheryl still didn't sit up, but I had the peace and help of God to cope with the problems.

'I thought everything was going to be alright after that. My relationship with God was mended. But one day in church the minister said, "We have no right to question what God brings into our lives." I sat there fuming – really angry – thinking, "How dare you say that? You have two perfectly normal children. You don't know what it's like to be told your daughter is never going to be like other children." But then we started to sing,

It will be worth it all when we see Jesus,
It will be worth it all when we see Christ.
One glimpse of His dear face
All sorrow will erase;
So bravely run the race
'Till we see Christ.

'And then God broke down the bitterness of my heart as I realised once more that God had it all under control.'

Towards the end of Cheryl's second year and after months of nursing her through a bad attack of measles, Catherine was worn out emotionally and physically, but she was putting her hopes in a visit to an eye specialist.

'I was trying to be positive. I was really confident that Cheryl's eyesight would be alright.'

But a brief examination from the specialist shattered Catherine's hopes. She was told by the specialist that the eye centres of Cheryl's brain had not developed, which left Catherine stunned. She felt all alone in the world, and just sat and cried. And then said, 'That's it, God; we're finished. I don't want any more to do with you. We'll look after our daughter ourselves. We don't need you!'

Catherine felt she could take no more. Cheryl could not walk or talk, she had epilepsy as well as a twisted back. But now her mother was told that she would never be able to see. She was diagnosed with microcephaly. As she pushed her little daughter in her pushchair everyone seemed to brush by her. She walked through the rain to the car where Philip was waiting.

'I yelled at him. "That's it. God doesn't care. I just can't take any more."'

Philip didn't reply, but as Catherine sat in the back of the car 'It was as if God whispered in my ear, "Fear not, I am with you." It was as if someone was talking to me: like a big bucket of peace being poured over me. God was saying He was with me.'

A Bible verse that had been precious to her as a teenager came back to her: 'Fear not, I have redeemed you; I have called you by my name; You are Mine. When you pass through the waters, I will be with you; And through the rivers, they shall not overflow you. When you walk through the fire, you shall not be burned, Nor shall the flame scorch you' (Isaiah 43:1–2, NKJV). That has been the key lesson Catherine and Philip have learned through Cheryl – not that God takes away all their problems and difficulties, but He is right there with them in the crisis. He gives them peace on the inside although life on the outside doesn't always seem to make sense.

> Should we not learn to trust Him
> Who knows all things best?
> And then whate'er befalls us
> We'll still have peace and rest.

'In fact, God has used Cheryl to introduce us to others with whom we can share the love of Christ. She has drawn out love from many and opened opportunities to share with others in similar circumstances,' says Philip.

In November 1981 Philip and Catherine had a baby boy, Paul. He was perfectly normal. Three and a half years later in July 1985 they had a third child, another daughter. There was real elation that they now had a healthy boy and girl. They were so delighted they named her Joy. They were told that all was well with her and she was strong.

But after about six weeks, the paediatrician told Catherine that Joy had the same condition as Cheryl and that things would probably go the same way that they did for Cheryl. Once again the family was devastated. They cried to God, asking Him why, and what more was there to learn when they had learned so much from Cheryl. They wondered why they had to learn all this again, and found it hard to see God's purpose and plans.

The church to which they belonged loved and supported them throughout this trying period. But after the shock wore off the pressure just mounted. People prayed for God's help for Philip and Catherine, and God answered in so many ways; but they still felt a lack of confidence in themselves. Having two severely handicapped girls under the age of six was more than they could cope with. Catherine didn't find it easy to share all she was going through with others. She realised she had to seek the Lord herself. Again Scripture verses and Christian poems were helpful to her. Catherine keeps a book of all the things which have been a blessing to her. She often opens it and reminds herself of the good which God has for her. At that time the hymn which encouraged her was:

Oh safe to the Rock that is higher than I
My soul in its conflicts and sorrows would fly.
So weary, so sinful
Thine, thine would I be
Thou blest Rock of Ages
I'm hiding in Thee.

Philip and Catherine have found that their Christian character has grown through all these pressures. Catherine has found that every failure is an experience to teach us something new, and therefore it is important to use each failure. Again, a familiar Bible verse sums up what she was learning at this time: '[T]hose who wait on the LORD Shall renew their strength; They shall mount up with wings like eagles, They shall run and not be weary, They shall walk and not faint' (Isaiah 40:31, NKJV).

In December 1989 Cheryl was in hospital for a week with double pneumonia. Early one Sunday morning the telephone rang. The night sister told Philip that just moments before Cheryl had died. Philip walked back up the stairs, woke Catherine and, believing that God takes to Himself children who die, told her that their little girl had gone Home. They were very sad days. But they have a hope and confidence which doesn't come with a set of easy answers. They have learned that God wants to be involved in the hurts and heartaches of life, and He doesn't stop pouring out His peace.

'It's as if I go from one hurdle to the next, but I'm glad that I have God to help me over those hurdles. I have my weepy days, but that shows I am human,' says Catherine.

'Some say there is no hope, but Cheryl had a purpose and a

quality in her life that God gave her. We saw God's plans being worked out in her wee life. People don't like to think about death and heaven, but God has shown me there is so much more to look forward to. Her life wasn't worthless. She had been very precious to us and I would not have changed the real Cheryl.'

Philip continues, 'We are sustained knowing that Cheryl is with Christ, which is far better. Down here she could not walk, now she is walking the streets of glory. Down here she could not see, but now she is looking upon the face of Jesus. Down here she could not talk, but now she is singing the praises of Christ. We could not keep going without the help of God: He is our refuge and strength, a very present help in times of trouble. God has His purpose in all these things even though we may not see it now.'

When they sat in the funeral car on the way to the cemetery there came over them a great peace such as they had never experienced before. In the service the preacher spoke from Isaiah 40:11, '[God] will feed His flock like a shepherd; He will gather the lambs with His arm, And carry them in His bosom, And gently lead those who are with young' (NKJV). God met with Philip and Catherine and has continued to meet them in their need.

Some years later Joy also died. Cheryl was 10, and Joy 13 years of age.

As they journeyed through the heartache of caring for and losing two daughters, they did not realise how God was preparing them for a much wider Christian ministry which was to extend across the world. Today they live in the beautiful Northern Ireland town of Coleraine near Giant's Causeway on the north coast.

Philip is now the minister of Coleraine Congregational Church. Catherine is involved in ministry to women in speaking, writing and pastoral situations. Since 2008 she has been writing books which have been best-sellers. Her latest is called, *When we can't, God can*, though she has recently been writing her first novel. Catherine's interest in writing started in primary school when she won a National School's Story Competition by the chocolate company, Cadbury. Her books reflect all that she has been through and powerfully speak to many.

Family is still vitally important to them. Their son, Paul, is married to Susie; they are both professional musicians. (See www.studio.orchestrations.com.) They have a son and daughter – grandchildren to Philip and Catherine.

CHAPTER 14

'TIL DEATH US DO PART
THE STORY OF SUSAN SAHL

The LORD will command His lovingkindness in the daytime, And in the night His song shall be with me – A prayer to the God of my life. (Psalm 42:8, NKJV)

At the age of 26, Susan Sahl's life was turned upside down when her young husband died without any warning. Susan had been converted to Christ as a teenager, but Martin's sudden death was to be the fiercest test of her faith.

She was a student at Leeds University when one autumnal day, during her final year, she was wandering pensively along a deserted street kicking up the fallen leaves. As she scrunched along she began to pray that by that time next year she would have met her future husband, and added almost frivolously that he must enjoy kicking up leaves in autumn. Little did Susan realise how significant this prayer was to become.

Almost a year later her prayer was answered in what she felt was a miraculous way. She had been helping on a beach mission in Cromer where she met a young man named Martin Sahl, though he was known affectionately to his friends as Mart. He was intelligent, witty and sincere. He had a first-class degree from Cambridge and yet she found he was not one of those who was keen to tell you so. He was genuinely humble. As they talked, Susan was taken by the wisdom and gentleness of this young man. By the end of the Mission they knew they had not seen the last of each other.

The following week they met in Cambridge and, sitting on a bench in Emmanuel College garden, they prayed together. As they said their 'Amens' Mart glanced at a beautiful tree above them, one small patch of which was turning amber. Mart looked at Susan and said, 'I love kicking up leaves in autumn, don't you?' She said nothing, but was clear in her mind that their relationship should be allowed to flourish!

It was not long before they began to see each other on a regular basis. Every weekend Martin commuted from London, where he was training to be a Chartered Accountant, to Leicester University where Susan had embarked on a teacher training course. During the week they wrote to each other daily in what was a rich form of communication and a way in which they learned to share every aspect of their lives with each other. Over the next year they spent hours in deep conversation, until they felt that there was nothing that they did not know about each other.

Susan continues her story: 'I don't think that Martin really needed to ask me to marry him, as we simply couldn't imagine having to be apart. The following year we chose an engagement ring and arranged a trip to Cromer, where God had first brought us together, and there Mart proposed to me. I said, "Yes" (of course!) and promptly burst into tears!'

The months to come were action-packed as they bought a house, decorated it, tamed the wild jungle of a garden, whilst making copious plans for a spring country wedding. They loved the wedding day, both feeling that it was the best day of their lives. God blessed those first months of their marriage so that they soon felt that they had been married for ever.

The following year, though, several major issues impinged on their happiness. Amongst them was the death of Susan's grandmother and the impending death of a close friend of hers who was suffering from a brain tumour. Mart and Susan spent hours discussing the subject of death, which had come so close, and how they felt about it. Times were tough in the City too, and Mart found himself facing the prospect of redundancy. This caused a lot of pain, forcing them to look carefully at their finances. Mart was able to plan how they could survive on her salary alone. Little did Susan know how significant these seemingly unfair events were to be in terms of preparing her for the tragedy which lay ahead.

As Christmas approached they made arrangements to see as many of their family and friends as they could. They spent Christmas Day at Susan's family home in Hertfordshire and then travelled to Dorking to spend time with Martin's family. As 27 December drew to a close they said goodbye to Martin's parents, as they were due to leave early the following morning, and retired happily to bed. At about 5.20am Susan was woken suddenly by Mart having a nightmare. She flicked on the bedside light and called out his name whilst shaking him by the shoulder, but he continued to thrash around, making a strange groaning noise.

'I knew instantly that something was wrong,' Susan recalls. 'Praying to God as I ran, I dashed into his sister's room for help. When we returned Mart had stopped thrashing around. Together we put him into the recovery position and Deborah ran to awaken their parents and call for an ambulance. I sat on the bed next to Mart, but by now his breathing pattern had changed; he was not breathing as frequently as he should have been. Then I heard one long expulsion of air, and Mart's body went limp. At that moment Mart's parents rushed in. We frantically tried to find a pulse, but there was none! Immediately we lifted his body to the floor and began mouth-to-mouth and pulmonary resuscitation. Despite my first-aid training, nothing could have prepared me for the shock and trauma of desperately trying to resuscitate my own husband.'

It seemed like an age, but was in fact only a few minutes before the ambulance crew arrived and took over from them. Susan was in a fog of confusion, so many thoughts were flashing through her mind. The heart monitor did not show a horizontal line but one with intermittent peaks and troughs, which made her wonder why Mart still appeared to be unconscious. Knowing they would soon have to go to hospital, she quickly pulled on some clothes, and then while Mart was being taken to the ambulance she hurriedly rang her parents for moral and prayerful support in the crisis. Her father answered the phone and she incoherently screamed, 'Dad, Mart's stopped breathing and they are trying to resuscitate him. I've got to go to hospital. Please pray!' It was such a garbled message for parents to receive at 5.25 in the morning.

Susan wanted to be allowed to travel to the hospital with Mart but they wouldn't let her. They followed the ambulance through the freezing fog, stopping at one point in the middle of the road as another ambulance flagged down Mart's to provide extra medical supplies. From the roadside all she could see were Mart's feet poking out of a red blanket, but Susan felt utterly helpless. Words failed her. She frantically tried to pray, but found it hard to string a coherent sentence together.

As soon as they arrived at the hospital they were ushered into a corridor. She still wanted to be with Mart but once again was barred from being with him. Martin's family went and sat in a small waiting room but Susan wanted to be alone, so she sat on the floor in the corridor. Feeling numb she prayed, fighting back tears and holding her head in a sense of disbelief at the awfulness of the situation. Shortly afterwards a nurse came and told them that things looked very grim. Desperately she prayed again, 'God, if we can't have Mart back as he was, will you take him and look after him; but if you do, we will need your help!'

Recounting what happened next, Susan says, 'About five minutes later the doctors came and told us that despite all their efforts Mart had died. I couldn't believe it. I felt shocked to the core, empty, numb, but painfully aware of the tragedy which had befallen us. When eventually I was allowed to see Mart I knew at once that this was just his earthly shell; he looked so peaceful that I could hardly believe that he was dead. The full horror of the situation had not yet had a chance to sink in.

I desperately needed space and solitude in which to pray and think things through.

'As the automatic door clicked open and I stepped outside, a feeling of stunned emptiness pervaded my very being. I stared in utter disbelief at the new day, crisp and frozen like my heart. I slumped exhaustedly beside a wall, tears were streaming down my face. Quietly I began to pray, "Father, you've taken the most precious thing in my life; please look after him. I feel so vulnerable, small and helpless. I desperately need your help." I sat alone in the semi-darkness until I felt strong enough to return to the hospital.'

Soon came the gruelling task of identifying the body. There were big questions shooting through her mind. At the age of 26, and after just 20 months of marriage, Susan was a widow. There had been no warning, so what had gone wrong? It doesn't cross your mind that when you kiss your spouse goodnight that he won't be alive by the morning. Susan knew too that she would want to say goodbye to Mart's earthly shell. Gently stroking his face and kissing his forehead, she whispered, 'Goodnight my darling. I love you.' Finally she ran her hands through his thick dark hair for the last time and turned to leave the room. Her heart was breaking, and she felt so lonely she wanted her life to end there and then.

But she recalls, 'Through the coming hours and days I had a very real sense of God sustaining me. It may sound strange, but I felt the tangible presence of God's warm reassuring hand on me.' At first Susan, who loved to sing, was unable to, but eventually her vocal ability came back and the first song she sang was 'Give thanks with a grateful heart'.

The day of the funeral was very difficult. Mart's earthly resting place was to be in the grounds of the church where they had been married. Susan spoke at the funeral service and felt that God gave her 'a peace which passes all understanding', coupled with an inner strength enabling her to cope with the pressures of the day. 'God's presence filled that village church. The warmth, love and support of my family and friends were really tangible. When I stood to speak, I could hardly believe that it was me talking!'

It was several anguished weeks before they were told the cause of Martin's sudden death. The autopsy revealed that he had a floppy mitral valve which, together with sudden cardiac arrhythmia, had for some reason caused irreversible heart failure. 'God had called him home instantly without any suffering, graciously allowing those who loved him most to be with him at the time of his death.'

But life was not easy as Susan recalls: 'Despite my peace about Mart's eternal destiny, nothing could have prepared me for the utter desolation I was to feel. At times my grief was almost uncontrollable. I seemed to be enveloped by an all-pervading emptiness, the ferocity of which I had never experienced before. I was totally unprepared for the depths of loneliness in which I would be submerged. All my hopes and dreams had been shattered into a myriad of tiny pieces. Painful memories flooded back, each bearing a bitter sting of their own. It was as if all the things which had previously been most precious to me now cut like sharpened swords. I felt totally incomplete, as though a part of me had died. I had not reckoned on how often and unexpectedly this deep despair would raise its ugly head.

'The immense task ahead was simple in name but incredibly hard in practice. I somehow had to get my shattered life back on the rails. I felt weak and totally uncoordinated, almost as if I was recovering from a general anaesthetic. It was really hard to begin to take everything in, somehow my brain did not have a compartment labelled 'indescribable, unbelievable tragedy' into which all these events could neatly slot. It seemed so wrong to be a widow at 26. Only God could minister to the deep pain welling up within me. Each tearful torrent was followed by a deep sense of His being in control of the situation, if only I would allow Him to be. In the face of real anguish, prayer seemed the only meaningful thing left in my life. My relationship with God was my lifeline. Despite everything, my life was in God's hands.'

Quite independently of each other, several friends spoke reassuringly to Susan, and also wrote one particular Bible verse which they believed was a promise from God to her. Taken from Jeremiah 29, God was speaking to His people, "For I know the plans I have for you", declares the Lord, "plans to prosper you and not to harm you, plans to give you hope and a future.' Somehow she began to see that there was going to be a future worth living.

Gradually she came to realise that 'Martin's life was not cut short, but completed', therefore there was also a purpose to her own sufferings. C.S. Lewis' idea that pain is God's megaphone to rouse a deaf world was helpful to her. It seemed that God was clearly teaching her through her suffering. 'When everything in my life had been removed, my relationship with God began to flourish. I had had years of half-listening to God, and half-following, but now in my darkest night Jesus was standing holding the lamp which would light my path, if only I would walk beside Him and not head off into the darkness alone. Through my suffering God was speaking very clearly to me from the Bible. A passage from the Good News translation of the Bible in particular was a great strength to me:

Do not cling to events of the past, or dwell on what happened long ago. Watch for the new thing that I am going to do, it is happening already – you can see it now! I will make a road through the wilderness and give you streams of water there. (Isaiah 43:18–19)

As time wore on, the intensity of pain began to fade. At each step of the way God proved Himself to be a very present help, gently guiding her and showing her the way ahead. God gave her a future and a hope, healing her aching heart and giving strength to somehow take another step forward towards inner healing and wholeness. 'I know that I could never have survived this year without God's help; the measure of healing is remarkable, and whilst the journey still goes on, I know that I will never walk alone.'

CHAPTER 15

THE GREAT DIVIDE

Jesus said: 'O Jerusalem, Jerusalem, the one who kills the prophets and stones those who are sent to her! How often I wanted to gather your children together, as a hen gathers her chicks under her wings, but you were not willing!' (Matthew 23:37, NKJV)

The shining thread which has run through many of these previous chapters has been the certain conviction that the sufferings of this present world will be more than compensated for by the joy and glory which are promised to people who have put their trust in Jesus. For the Christian, to be with the Saviour throughout eternity will be heaven in itself. So it is important to ask ourselves whether we are absolutely sure that we share that certainty of our future destiny.

Throughout history there has been a basic divide between people which is not based on sex, colour, people group, economic situation, or even whether a person has suffered. The issue is whether the person has come to know the true and living God. Not only does that impact what happens after death, but it is that relationship with God that transforms the attitudes we have towards every experience of life. The Christian has many reasons to react very differently to the unbeliever to all that life throws at them.

First, *the believer has God to thank in times of joy.* This book has focused on difficulties, but most people have times of great happiness and joy. So who does one thank when gazing on a beautiful sunset, or enjoying a fine meal, or spending time with a dearly loved friend? Who do you thank for the beauty and wonder of creation, whether looking around at the world, looking in the depths of the oceans, or the vastness of space?

The story is told of two French revolutionaries in 1789 who boasted to a Christian that they would tear down every reminder of God. 'Oh,' asked the believer, 'and what will you do about the stars?'

The Bible is full of people who found reasons to praise God. When Moses had led the people of Israel across the Red Sea and their enemies had been defeated, he proclaimed, 'I will sing to the LORD, for he is highly exalted. The horse and the rider he has hurled into the sea' (Exodus 15:1). Centuries later, after the building of the first temple in Jerusalem had been completed, King Solomon praised God saying, 'Praise be to the LORD, the God of Israel, who with his own hand has fulfilled what he promised with his own mouth to my father David' (1 Kings 8:15). Later still, Daniel, after his deliverance from the lions' den could say, 'My God sent His angel and shut the lions' mouths, so that they have not hurt me ' (Daniel 6:22, NKJV). In the Bible there is a collection of 150 songs of praise in the book we call 'The Psalms'. They are full of praise to God. The theme of gratitude and praise continues in the New Testament part of the Bible, so that both Peter in prison, and Paul in a storm at sea, found strength in praising God. We read in the Bible's last book – Revelation – that praise is the great anthem of heaven for all eternity.

American Colonel James Irwin is one of a very small group of people who have walked on the moon. He wrote about his experiences:

I felt very special when I looked at my footprints on the moon. Scientists said that they would be there for a million years. Looking up I could see the earth, the size of a marble. It was so beautiful and so far away, and yet I felt strangely at home. When our mission returned I thanked the men who designed and built our spacecraft, those who helped to operate the systems during our trip, those dear friends around the world who had prayed for our success, and I thanked God for allowing us to leave the earth and explore a portion of His heavens.[8]

Secondly, *the believer has God to turn to in times of trouble*. All of us are aware that we depend on other people, yet strangely, along with this sense of dependency, those in need are conscious of a sense of alienation from other people. Just as we can approach a monarch only on certain conditions, so too often we can approach others only when

---

[8] Irwin, James. *Footprints on the Moon*. Available at: http://www.christianheritagemins.org/articles/Footprints%20on%20the%20Moon.pdf

everything is right for us. We often feel we cannot share our needs with them.

There is a Russian fable which tells of a 'hospitable' householder who used to tell the local villagers that they would be welcome at any time in his large house for food and warmth. Nobody ever came though, because he had two large Alsatians roaming around his grounds!

By contrast, Jesus is available to all who will come to Him. He welcomes all: the unloved, the unlovely and the apparently unlovable. We read in the Bible that 'the common people heard Him gladly' (Mark 12:37, NKJV) but with them came the despised, the deprived and the sinful, and none were turned away. He was described by others as 'the friend of sinners', and He said of His mission that He had 'come to seek and to save the lost'.

Jesus invites all to come to Him with the loveliest of words, 'Come to Me, all you who labour and are heavy laden, and I will give you rest. Take My yoke upon you and learn from Me, for I am gentle and lowly in heart, and you will find rest for your souls. For My yoke is easy and My burden is light.' (Matthew 11:28–30, NKJV). Jesus encourages us to come to Him just as we are. He doesn't ask us to improve ourselves, clean up our act or make ourselves worthy of Him, but simply invites us to come to Him with the needs that only He can meet. So the Christian is the person who has heard and answered that call, and knows that Jesus Christ is the only one who can satisfy the person's greatest need.

Thirdly, *the believer has God to trust in life and death.* Everyone has decisions to make, difficulties to face and despondency to overcome. Because He not only lived and died, but was buried and rose from the dead, Jesus is now the living, loving, personal Saviour to all who trust Him. The Bible describes Jesus as 'the Saviour of all men, and especially of those who believe' (1 Timothy 4:10).

Because of this we are encouraged to cast all our care upon Him, because He cares for us. He not only cares, but He can cope with us! We read in the Bible's Book of Proverbs (3:5-6), 'Trust in the LORD with all your heart And lean not on your own understanding; In all your ways acknowledge Him, And He shall direct your paths' (NKJV). We have seen in the stories in the preceding chapters that however awful the circumstances may be through which God's people have to pass, His eye is always on the thermometer – He knows the heat of what we are enduring; His eye is always on the clock – He knows how long the suffering should endure; and His eye is always on the barometer – He knows the pressure we can bear. For everyone who trusts Him there is always the promise of God's eternal presence. Jesus said to His followers, 'I am with you always, even to the end of the age'. (Matthew 28:20, NKJV). God had said the same centuries before to Moses' successor, Joshua, "I will not leave you nor forsake you.' (Joshua 1:5, NKJV). God goes before His people: He is behind them; He is above and below them, and He even abides with them. And this is for eternity.

The Bible teaches that after death there is judgement. Every religion leads to God. Even the atheist is on a journey to meeting God. The big question is whether we will meet God as our judge or as our Saviour who welcomes us. The God who made us has the absolute right to either welcome us to His heavenly home or sentence us to hell. To be saved from hell, we need someone who can forgive us and rescue us from all that condemns us. For it is our sin that brings us into judgement. Sin is breaking God's commandments; it is falling short of all that God is; it is not loving God with all our hearts, minds, souls and strength, and not loving our neighbours as we love ourselves.

All sin is primarily against God. That is why it is His forgiveness that we need. Sir James Simpson, Scottish scientist and discoverer of chloroform, among other things, said that the greatest discovery of his life was that he was a sinner in need of a Saviour. Jesus Christ is the only perfectly qualified Saviour. Because He never sinned He did not need forgiveness. And because He is God incarnate – God clothed in humanity – He was able to live a perfect life, and then go to the cruel suffering of a cross where He hung as a common criminal paying for the sins of the world. 'God was in Christ reconciling the world to Himself ' (2 Corinthians 5:19, NKJV). Jesus was dying the death we all deserve, for our sin was laid on Him. He was providing the one and only way to forgiveness and a relationship with the true and living God.

It is because Jesus died for us, then triumphantly rose from the dead three days later, conquering all that conquers us, that He can deal with our future. Life here on earth is temporary and short. There is an old fable about a man who made an unusual agreement with Death. He told the Grim Reaper that he would willingly accompany him when the time came to die, but on one condition – that Death would send a messenger well in advance to warn him. Weeks turned into months, and months into years. Then one bitter winter evening, as the man sat alone thinking about all his worldly possessions, Death suddenly entered the room and tapped him on the shoulder. The man was startled and cried out in despair, 'You're here so soon and without warning. I thought we made an agreement.' Death replied, 'I've more than kept my part. I've sent you many messengers. Look at yourself in the mirror and you'll see some of them.' As the man complied, Death whispered, 'Notice your hair, once it was thick and black, but now it is thin and white. Look at the way you turn your head to listen to my voice because you can no longer hear well. Observe how closely you get to the mirror in order to see yourself clearly. Yes, I've sent my messengers through the years. I've kept my part of the bargain. It is too bad that you did not keep yours. I'm sorry that you are not ready for me, but the time has come for you to leave.'

Someone has mathematically calculated a schedule that compares the average lifetime with a single day beginning at 7am. If your age is:

15, the time is 10.25am
25, the time is 12.42pm
35, the time is 3.00pm
45, the time is 5.16pm
55, the time is 7.34pm
65, the time is 9.55pm
75, the time is 11.00pm

Jesus has tasted death for each one of us and defeated death and the grave. This very day, if you will turn from your sin in repentance and by faith trust Him to be your Lord and Saviour, He will forgive you and by His Holy Spirit come to live within you.

Jesus said, '[A]nd the one who comes to Me I will by no means cast out' (John 6:37, NKJV).

When you put your trust in Jesus, He clears all the past and strengthens you to serve and obey Him as He guides you through your future. Many have found that praying in words similar to those below has helped them in the act of putting their trust in Jesus. Will you pray like this now?

Heavenly Father,

Thank you that you know all there is to know about me. I confess to You my sin and want to repent of it. Please forgive me. Thank You that Jesus died for me, and that He rose again from the dead. Please come to live in my life and become my Lord and Saviour, helping me to follow You. Thank You for loving me.

I pray in Jesus' name.

Amen.

If you are sincere and serious about trusting God, you will have peace with Him, and throughout your life, the peace of God. One day you will enjoy eternal peace which God has promised to all who belong to Him.

If you have prayed this prayer for the first time, please email me so that I can send some booklets to help you mature in your Christian faith.

roger@rogercarswell.com

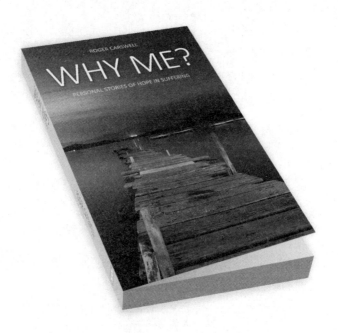

10Publishing is the publishing house of 10ofThose.
It is committed to producing quality Christian
resources that are biblical and accessible.

www.10ofthose.com is our online retail arm selling
thousands of quality books at discounted prices.

For information contact: **info@10ofthose.com**
or check out our website: **www.10ofthose.com**